Ex Libris

a gift of the Episcopal Church Women, 1992

A Hillspeak Bookplate · Printed in Eureka Springs, Arkansas

New Millennium, New Church

Trends Shaping the
Episcopal Church
for the
Twenty-first Century

Richard Kew ✠ *Roger J. White*

COWLEY PUBLICATIONS
Cambridge ✦ Boston
Massachusetts

Published in the United States of America by Cowley Publications, a division of the Society of St. John the Evangelist. No portion of this book may be reproduced, stored in or introduced into a retrieval system, or transmitted, in any form or by any means—including photocopying—without the prior written permission of Cowley Publications, except in the case of brief quotations embodied in critical articles and reviews.

International Standard Book Number: 1-56101-063-4 (cloth), 1-56101-062-6 (paper)
Library of Congress Number: 92-10806

Library of Congress Cataloging-in-Publication Data

Kew, Richard, 1945 -
   New millennium, new church : trends shaping the Episcopal Church for the twenty-first century / Richard Kew, Roger J. White.
      p. cm.
   ISBN 1-56101-063-4 (alk. paper). — ISBN 1-56101-062-6 (pbk. : alk. paper)
   1. Episcopal Church. I. White, Roger, 1941- . II. Title.
BX5933.K48 1992
283'.73'0112—dc20   92-10806

 This book is printed on recycled, acid-free paper and was produced in the United States of America.

Cowley Publications
28 Temple Place
Boston, Massachusetts 02111

We dedicate this book
to our wives,
Pru and Rosemary,
for sharing us with the Church

and

to all those who have journeyed with us
and so played a part in the writing of this book

and

to the praise and glory of God

Acknowledgments

*T*his book began in a place neither of us could ever find again in the middle of Louisiana! We were both present at a day with the clergy of the Diocese of Western Louisiana in December 1990 at their diocesan camp—and so began an exchange of ideas. We would like to thank the bishop and clergy of Western Louisiana for their contribution.

We would also like to thank SPCK and the Diocese of Milwaukee for permitting us time to develop these ideas and get them down on paper. We are especially grateful for the hard work of Barbara Klauber of Bishop White's staff, and the hours she spent preparing manuscripts and diskettes.

To our many friends and acquaintances who encouraged, counseled and advised us, we offer our deepest appreciation. Even to those sceptics who did not think we had it in us, we say thank you.

Cynthia Shattuck, editor of Cowley Publications, is to be commended for her confident enthusiasm that these ideas could be developed into a book that would serve the Episcopal Church as it tries to focus on its future.

We thank our wives and families for their patience and understanding of two men who already spend too much time away from home, and then disappear to a coastal resort to write! However, Hilton Head Island proved a stimulating environment to swim, walk the beach, eat seafood, and birth this book.

The Authors

Table of Contents

How to Use this Book

This book is intended to be a compass for the 1990s, not a detailed road map. Its task is to help you find the way forward, not give precise details of how to get there. We hope you will use it to help yourselves, the parishes, dioceses, and other Episcopal Church institutions of which you are part to plan effectively for the days ahead. Good planning helps focus an organization and minimize waste of time and resources; understanding the trends shaping the future help with that process. This will be one facet of a fruitful exercise as you prepare for the future: it is not a "spoon-fed" formula for success.

What we have attempted to do is provide discussion highlights with each trend outlined, which we hope you will use as you involve yourself in this process of planning. Education and recruitment of as many people as possible will be important for this process.

We recognize that Episcopalians are often spread thinly, and certain of these trends will be more relevant in some parts of the USA than others. The Church in New England is very different from the Midwest and the South, for example.

In addition, it is vital that groups using this book of trends gather local data to further inform their planning process. Our trends give an idea what might be going on inside the Church, but they then need to be anchored within the local environment, which is social, cultural, economic, ethnic, and geographical. Such considerations will make your planning more effective, and reduce the likelihood of missing local variations that might be important pieces in the puzzle for your parish. The information to be collated and taken into consideration in this planning process could be drawn from the following sources:

✚ Census data and demographic information

✚ Planning materials being used by local, county, and state governments

✚ Information that other churches may have used in their planning processes. Be certain you gather it all: Catholic, mainline Protestant, evangelical, Pentecostal, and fundamentalist. *Episcopalians have a temptation to be selective in their use of church data, just gathering it from churches whose theology, polity, and style they like; overcome this temptation!*

✚ Insights from business, commerce, the education community, human and health care services, etc.

✚ Information that sets your community in the international context: exports, student exchanges, linkages between ethnic Americans and their land of origin, multinational corporations, etc.

Above all, pray for divine insight and discernment. Such prayers can be part of our own daily devotions and parish prayer groups specifically established to support the planning process. Effective planning is dependent upon the wise use of good data, and our minds are made more sensitive to God's will only as we open ourselves to God's directing. We would suggest the following adaptation of Prayer 12, found on page 818 in the Book of Common Prayer:

> Almighty and everliving God, source of all wisdom and understanding, be present with us as we take counsel to plan for the effective ministry of our (parish, diocese, school, agency, etc.) in the days ahead, and for the renewal and mission of your Church. Teach us in all things to seek first your honor and glory. Guide us to perceive what is right, and grant us both the courage to pursue it and the grace to accomplish it; through Jesus Christ our Lord. *Amen.*

While we think we have identified some major trends reshaping the Episcopal Church today, we do not suffer from the illusion that we possess 20/20 foresight. We are certain we have misread details; only time will show us which they are. We think we have understood the major thrusts to bear in mind during the next decade. But the world is changing so radically and rapidly that extraordinary events are likely to remake circumstances. The thirteen trends we have outlined in the following pages provide a snapshot of the Church as it was in the latter part of 1991, although by the time this book is published things will have begun to alter. The secret is to be able to gauge when certain trends begin to peter out, others emerge, and still others transform themselves into something significantly different.

As a diocesan bishop whose ministry reaches beyond his diocesan boundaries, and as the director of the American wing of the world's oldest mission agency, we have been able to travel widely and observe what has been happening in the Church both at home and overseas. Between us we have over thirty-five years of ministry in the Episcopal Church, but as transplanted Englishmen, Alistair Cooke-like, we have a vantage point from which we can stand back and analyze the train of events relatively objectively. Roger White was reared in the Anglo-Catholic tradition, and has a broader theological perspective than Richard Kew's formation in the evangelical arm of Anglicanism. We have used our differing perspectives to balance the other's perceptions—not without the occasional disagreement.

In the course of watching and thinking, we have identified thirteen trends we believe will shape the Episcopal Church during the next generation. Many of these have parallels in the other historical Christian traditions in this country, while some are uniquely our own and we perceive to be God's gift to our Church. While the unexpected will certainly happen and some of these points will require reworking, we are confident that most of these concepts will play an important part in directing the flow of our lives as Episcopalians for a number of years to come.

As we have defined these trends, we have interfaced them with wide-ranging reading of the secular and religious press. We have digested a broad variety of books, newsletters, and reports, and we are addicted to TV and radio news, and commentary on the news, current affairs, and finance. None of our trends can be seen in isolation. Our identification of certain trends does not necessarily mean we personally affirm the issues and ideas behind them all. All we are saying is that they are there, and whether we agree or disagree, they are likely to influence and direct the Church's future. Therefore, as we plan and strategize, they *must* be taken into account.

We have sought to understand the flow of American society and culture as it impacts the life of the Christian community and acts as the backdrop for the drama of living out the faith. We truly believe that if this Church heeds these trends and learns to read the signs of the times, it will be in a position to influence this nation and the world for the good, moving us to fulfill our call as the people of Christ by living out what we profess to believe.

CHAPTER ONE

Setting the Scene

*H*ave you heard the liturgy that echoes round the Episcopal Church? In our travels round the country we often hear it. It opens with the words, "The Church is in deep trouble," and continues with certain rituals: frowning, head shaking, sighing, and tongue-clicking, to name but a few. The invariable homily usually focuses on the latest abuse of power by a "rogue bishop," an expression of unbelief by a publicity-seeking theologian, or the inconsistencies in the life of the rector, the rector's spouse, even the rector's dog!

We've described this liturgy to friends in all the other mainline churches and find they have something similar, whether they be Lutheran, Presbyterian, Methodist, Roman Catholic, or members of the United Church of Christ. While the good news is often passed over, there is no smoke without fire. Whether we like it or not, there is substance behind these words. Like us, these other Christians have good reason to be concerned for the future of their own churches.

We should not be surprised, for we are in the midst of a major revolution in the life of American Christianity. This is especially true in the "mainline Protestant denominations," an umbrella term used to describe the historic American churches, including the Episcopal Church (which tends to fit uncomfortably into this bracket). All of us who fall into this broad category are being "re-formed," although for the most part we would rather not recognize or acknowledge the revolution that is taking place.

Recently, John Mulder, a leading Presbyterian historian and seminary dean, defined the circumstances before all of us:

> We are living in one of the most exciting, fascinating, and significant periods in all of American religious history. Our situation has more similarity with the late eighteenth and early nineteenth centuries than it does with the period since World War II. Today is an era of the re-forming and re-definition of American Protestantism and American religious life, just as it was during the revolutionary and early national periods of American history. It is not yet clear what these changes are going to produce for American religious life or for our denominations. But some trends are now becoming clear.[1]

The Presbyterian Church has been the subject of an encyclopedic five-year study funded by the Lilly Endowment, on the present state and the future of these churches.[2] The report is chock full of pertinent lessons not only for Presbyterians but for the Episcopal Church as well, as we wrestle with the raging currents that are reshaping our church life. We ignore these lessons at our peril.

Most of the trends now facing us are not brand new; they started to emerge following World War II, but burst forth most evidently during the 1960s. It is not difficult to trace their roots much further back, into the late nineteenth and the early years of the current century. The diverse origins of these trends demonstrate the complexity of the situation in which we find ourselves, and therefore we cannot anticipate a single quick fix as we face the challenge of the future.

The Situation to be Confronted

What the Lilly Endowment study reveals is that the mainline churches have lost the recognition the culture once gave them. The Episcopal Church, like the other major traditions, is no longer looked to as an important moral influence shaping American society. One example of this is that in many parts of the country the office of the clergy no longer receives the support and respect it was once given. In his enthronement sermon in April 1991, the Archbishop of Canterbury, George L. Carey, explained this similar paradigm shift as it has affected the English Church. He described the Church of England as a little old lady sitting in the corner of a room. When she speaks out against society's ills, people are respectful and pat her on the head, then they go away, ignoring her and all that she has said! The same response is increasingly true on this side of the Atlantic Ocean.

The ground rules have changed radically in our society, yet we still try to operate as though nothing has altered in the last fifty years. Episcopalians delude themselves that people still make "the social climb" as they progress through life from Baptist to Methodist, Presbyterian to Episcopalian. What Vance Packard once described in his book, *The Status Seekers*, as "The Long Road from Pentecostal to Episcopal" is a social movement now dead and gone, alive only in the vivid imagination and yearnings of Episcopalians who want to believe "as it was in the beginning, is now and ever shall be...."

These days, in the religious life of many communities in the North, it is the Roman Catholics who are "running the show," while the Baptist churches predominate in much of the South. Meanwhile, culturally and spiritually, there is more to keep conservative evangelicals in their churches than there used to be. A steady flow of new members and concomitant numerical growth is a result of the high priority they give to evangelism.

Honesty should bring us as Episcopalians to accept the consequences of our membership hemorrhage: 30% of all Episcopalians have disappeared since 1964, while the overall population of the United States has continued to increase. While the decline slowed in the 1980s and has either reached a plateau or been reversed in some places, we have little to be proud of. *The Anglican Digest* reported in 1991 that "Episcopal Church membership declined again for the 21st consecutive year. In 1989 the Church lost 22,009 members, the equivalent of closing ten of our largest parishes in one year."[3] Interestingly, US population growth began slowing in the mid-1960s, at the very time membership in the mainline churches started to slip. This suggests our loss is partly due to changed demographics, but we would be deluding ourselves if we hid behind this statistic. Neither should we pretend that most of our loss is "dead wood."

Baby boomers might be rediscovering the Christian faith in increasing numbers, but they have little loyalty to the church of their birth or upbringing. Their values are different from those of their parents, they are strongly anti-institutional, and when looking for a church seek *services and programs* for their children first. They also have a very acute sense of their own needs, and will not be content in a congregation that does not deliberately set out to meet them. Those who were raised in the Episcopal Church often "grow up" out of the Church and end up going nowhere. They join that swelling segment of our society that has opted for an entirely secular lifestyle with no church involvement whatsoever. Our most enthusiastic newer members are usually those raised in other Christian traditions, while a huge proportion of "cradle" Episcopalians just drop out. This speaks volumes about our education and formation, or lack of it! We have been a church in which it is easy to be baptized and confirmed, to become a "member." It has been relatively easy to join; it has been equally easy to leave. We have asked little of our members and in response they have given little in return, and have left unchallenged and certainly unconverted.

Mission is given a low priority. Decades have passed since we deliberately planned for new church growth. As our people move to newly built suburbs they have found relatively few Episcopal congregations to greet them. Unless something special is happening, city churches left behind either die or hang on by their "endowment fingertips." Those who leave rural churches for the suburbs fare no better than urbanites, because rural population decline has not been matched by the need for churches to serve the new residential areas to which this shifting population moves.

During times of decline, we can begin to learn the dynamics of growth. Except in unusual circumstances, growth comes in newly established congregations, which we have stopped developing for the most part, except in the Sun Belt and in a handful of farsighted dioceses.

A further example of our shortsightedness has been the de-emphasizing of campus ministry, the threshold over which the church's future leadership has so often passed. Interestingly, at the very time we were opting out of college student work, it became the major focus of conservative evangelical Christians and interdenominational bodies who poured into college ministry vast resources, giving campus work a high priority. It is little wonder that groups such as Inter-Varsity Christian Fellowship, Campus Crusade for Christ, and the Navigators thrive, while we have almost quit altogether.

As we have moved our emphasis to "causes and issues," away from the individual's relationship to God and the parish's relationship to God and to one another, we have experienced further decline. The "causes and issues"—civil rights, peace, liturgical renewal, the emerging role of women—were and are most worthy. But an "issue" is not necessarily a life-changing encounter with the risen Lord Jesus Christ. Issues do not convert people: they are the fruit of our meeting God and our wish to live out the Baptismal Covenant in the world. We are tempted to leap directly to the third stage of the Covenant, as it is laid out in the Book of Common Prayer (pp. 304-305), giving only passing acknowledgement to the other two: our response to God as we come face-to-face with him as our creator, savior, sustainer, and enthuser; and our need to be nourished in the life of the church by word, fellowship, sacrament, and prayers. Again, as we have side-stepped encounters with God, those from evangelical traditions have thrived in the vacuum left by ourselves and other mainline churches.

Furthermore, we have structures that thwart the natural and strong impetus toward focusing on the life of the congregation. Instead of using the resources of the diocese and the national church to support mission where the people are, in the parish, we have turned things upside down. The revolt against quotas and assessments to dioceses and to the national church is no accident.

Neither is it an accident that parishes tend to seek priests with substantial pastoral and preaching gifts, and that Episcopalians yearn for personal spiritual growth toward maturity. Congregations are desperately searching for clergy who are renewed, emphasizing and proclaiming the Gospel in word and deed. Some may find this threatening, but these are indications of hope, evidence of the emergence of a reinvigorated Church.

The truth is, "A church is only as big as it wants to be." Consciously or unconsciously, at local, diocesan, and national levels we have made the decision to shrink, have pursued policies that will guarantee it, and covered it up with high-sounding theological words like "prophetic witness." The time is long overdue to balance this with plans for the development of new congregations.

The Lilly Endowment study gives cause for thought; it could depress us if we were to let it, but it ought not to paralyze us. We need to face facts openly and honestly, and not brush them under the rug. We believe that thoughtful ownership of these discoveries is the point at which genuine renewal begins. There are already the seeds of life in those spots where the Church is seriously addressing this demise, and is planning to reverse three decades of "cruising" and living off the heritage of the past.

On Planning–Or Failing to Do So

One of the many talents of the English is their capacity to "muddle through." The Episcopal Church, in its sometimes misguided love affair with the authors' native land, too often attempts to emulate the British, usually with disastrous results. By their haphazardness, even the English miss a multitude of opportunities that come their way. We do not believe it is either godly, or biblical, or good stewardship of our resources to function without a long-term strategy and precise plan.

It seems clear from the Gospels that Jesus had a game plan for his ministry, and when he ascended into heaven he outlined an extension of it for his followers to flesh out what he had begun, once the Holy Spirit had descended upon them. "Go into all the world," he told them, "Beginning in Jerusalem, Judea and Samaria, then on to the very ends of the earth" (Acts 1:8). The Apostle Paul also took evangelism very seriously. His travels and letters paint a picture of a man developing a plan of action that, he hoped, would enable him to preach Christ where Christ had never been proclaimed before. The sheer size of his vision dwarfs us. At a time when travel was a hazardous and time-consuming business, he had the audacity to proclaim his "ambition to preach the gospel, not where Christ has already been named, lest I build on another man's foundation..." (Rom. 15:20).

If the Episcopal Church is once again to be a force to be reckoned with in American Christianity, then it is vital we seek forgiveness for past arrogance and begin developing challenging strategies and plans for local, national, and international ministry. These strategies should be framed within the context of discerning prayer and a willingness to be guided by the Holy Spirit, enabling us to address the needs of the world where Christ has placed us to be his people. We should heed and study the example of our Savior and his Apostles.

Too often the parameters of our long-range planning are triennial or limited by the extent of budget projections, which tend to dampen imagination and vision. Instead of trying to visualize what we want things to be like in three, five, or ten years, and then asking how we are to get there, we tend to be overwhelmed by immediate problems and difficulties.

At a national level, we seem to live from General Convention to General Convention. For those involved, that means planning and working for just three years between conventions, as commissions, usually given insufficient time, write a Blue Book report with a vision of where we may be going in the decade before us. Most of this hectic commission activity is done in two years, without scriptural or theological reflection, and is often very obviously devoid of any such basic premise, although our performance in this area is showing signs of improvement. At the grass-roots level, most parishes fumble around, their planning usually limited to what might happen next Sunday.

Instead, we need to encourage parishes, dioceses, the national church, seminaries, and other agencies of the Church to *strategize boldly*, to frame expansive plans, as if our souls depended on it—because they probably do. Dream dreams, have visions, and may our efforts and God's grace find ways to give them legs. Those who make no mistakes are the ones who lack the courage to launch out boldly into the future.

Framing strategies is hard work. It requires research, study, and prayer. Then as we shape these plans they need to be tested with more thought and research, and marinated richly in more prayer. And even when plans are in place, they aren't set in concrete. We need to be flexible and be prepared to return our strategies to the drawing board at a moment's notice as the realities around us alter. And how these realities are constantly changing! Our national church staff and structures are now a mere shadow of what they were a generation ago, while power and program have and will continue to shift to congregations, and to a lesser extent, to diocesan bodies.

Whether we like it or not, the future is coming to meet us at an accelerating pace. To be wise stewards of time, it is essential that we attempt to understand the trends shaping the era into which we are being projected. Using information available from the past and present, we are in a position to make calculated forecasts about the future. There are some who consider attempts at prediction faithless and "unspiritual," but the same folks will watch the weather forecast for days in advance, to make sure rain does not ruin the parish picnic. If they are prepared to observe trends in the weather for something relatively trivial, why not grapple with trends that can help them plan for effective ministry one, three, seven, or fifteen years down the road?

Yet grappling with trends does not mean the end of surprises. Tomorrow is far from predictable, and however good our plans and however faithful we are, God's agenda for mission will often confound us. But this does not exonerate us from making the attempt. Paul had his plans to take the Gospel to every corner of the Mediterranean world, yet the Almighty wanted him to witness to the resurrection of Jesus Christ before the emperor Nero. This surprising turn of events caused him great distress, and forced him to rewrite and reconsider his plans.

In recent years, we have witnessed the political transformation of the former Soviet Union and Eastern Europe: its suddenness has confounded the pundits. No sooner had the world begun to digest this and adjust to the consequences, than Iraq invaded Kuwait. A coalition of forces was given a United Nations mandate to liberate that tiny Persian Gulf nation, and we found ourselves embroiled in an unexpected high-tech war. What Alvin Toffler calls a "power shift" is taking place, one which will cause further surprises like these in coming years.

Even the sage who gathered the Proverbs reminds us of the tenuous nature of planning: "Humans plan their ways, but God directs their steps" (Prov. 16:9). But the probability of extraordinary lurches away from what appears to be a predictable course should not deter us from attempting to come to grips with trends, and thereby to enable effective strategies for mission and ministry. One of the messages our era is sending us is that our planning should be flexible, and we should be willing to make drastic changes as we work our way toward clear and stated goals.

A few years ago, Tom Sine, a leading Presbyterian trends analyst, told a gathering of missiologists, "If we can anticipate even a few of the trends, challenges, and needs, it provides us each time to create some new forms of strategic response."[4] If we surrender to the tides of history, and only acknowledge trends when they are sweeping us downstream, then not only will precious opportunities have been missed, but we will also see more and more of our efforts brought to nought.

Episcopalians have a tendency to look backward rather than forward, glorying in our heritage and doing things "the way they have always been done." While we value the rich-ness of our Anglican tradition as much as anyone, to yearn for a bygone era is a luxury we can no longer afford, if the Gospel is to be proclaimed "in word and deed" to this and future generations. We are compelled to shift gears into the future tense, taking the treasures of the past and translating them in such a way that they are relevant for today and tomorrow. Our heritage is worth little if it is meaningless to those with whom we are trying to communicate the truths of the Christian Gospel. George E. Barna shares similar thoughts when he writes,

> When God provides us with opportunities to foresee how to meet the needs of [those who search for the truth]— when He gives us glimpses of the future—it is to enable us to serve Him better not only in the future but by making smarter choices today!...By being forward-looking in our thinking, we can become effective change agents, rather than affected changed agents.[5]

In a talk to clergy in the Diocese of Milwaukee, Larry Ras-mussen said that if we are to plan for the future of the Church, it has both short- and very long-term implications. He calls us to be "planters of both pumpkin and date seeds." Pumpkin seeds will produce a rapid and amazingly fruitful crop, while if you plant date seeds it is unlikely that you will live to see fruit from a tree that takes so many years to ma-ture before it begins its useful life. But its fruit will serve another generation profusely. We are called to plan for both short- and long-term fruitfulness.

The plain questions before us in this generation are, Who is this Jesus we have chosen to follow? What can we affirm about the transforming Christ in the midst of our culture and plurality of religions of the world? What does Christ call us to be as the baptized—what makes us distinctive, what supports us in the community of faith, what vision of service and striving for justice and reconciliation do we discern and implement? What do we as Episcopalians have to offer as our distinctive contribution to the mission of God, as the Gospel is proclaimed to today's people and to generations yet to hear the Word, proclaimed in words and deeds?

CHAPTER TWO

Renewal Movements
Come of Age

*T*he media have always loved an ecclesiastical scandal. A few days before Easter 1960, the Episcopal Church provided them with a beauty. What better copy than the furor caused when the curate of a large congregation resigned publicly and stripped off his vestments as he stormed out of the church? The cause of the uproar was, of all things, the rector's Palm Sunday sermon.

The preacher professed no heresy, neither was he guilty of any misconduct, but it was to be his last Sunday as rector of the prosperous parish of St. Mark's, Van Nuys, California. The revelation made from the pulpit that morning was to reverberate around the Episcopal Church. For the first time, he told his congregation he had received a new infilling of the Holy Spirit, enabling him to speak in other tongues.

When the late Dennis Bennett's tongues-speaking came to the surface it signaled something new was beginning to happen in the Episcopal Church. While his was not the first example of "pentecostal phenomena" among Episcopalians, it certainly gained the most publicity. The whole uproar seems rather quaint more than thirty years later, when literally thousands of Episcopalians have had similar experiences. Today there are parishes where healings are commonplace, and no one thinks twice about prophecies and singing in tongues. Yet Bennett's *Nine O'Clock in the Morning* experience was the first inkling that the Episcopal Church was on the edge of an unfamiliar threshold. Since that time spiritual renewal in various incarnations has been gradually moving from the periphery toward the heart of the Church's daily life. We see no reason to think there will be a change of direction or momentum in coming years.

The Varieties of Renewal

In the last three decades, renewal has expressed itself not only in charismatic terms, but also in evangelical and Anglo-Catholic ones. Dennis Bennett became something of an outcast as he wrestled to make sense of his charismatic experience. But even as he moved to a tiny mission congregation in Seattle, a handful of future Episcopal leaders, seeking to supplement their theological education received at home, were enrolling in some of the evangelical seminaries of the Church of England. Meanwhile, a leading evangelical scholar, the late Philip E. Hughes, moved from Britain, engaged himself in the life of the Episcopal Church, and became a focus for Episcopalian evangelical activity. The seeds of a healthy evangelical renewal were being planted.

The Anglo-Catholic stream of Episcopal life was also being enriched through the introduction of the Cursillo movement into the Church. The "Biretta Belt" dioceses in Illinois and Wisconsin came to appreciate this successful program brought from Spain by the Roman Catholics. Taken over and adapted to suit the Anglican tradition, Cursillo played first in Peoria for these midwestern Episcopal dioceses. Anglo-Catholic renewal was given a further shot in the arm with the arrival of Michael Marshall, former Bishop of Woolwich, who established the Anglican Institute in St.

Louis, Missouri, in 1985. These strands of renewal have been particularly important to the vast majority of Anglo-Catholics for whom separation into schism or transfer to Rome are neither valid nor attractive options.

While there has been an increasingly close interrelationship and cross-fertilization between charismatic, evangelical, and Anglo-Catholic renewal, there are distinct differences in style and emphasis. Charismatics put greater emphasis on exercising the variety of gifts of the Holy Spirit, whereas evangelicals urge the Church and individual believers to put every aspect of their lives under the authority of Holy Scripture. On the other hand, Anglo-Catholic theology and practice appreciates the universality of the Church, and insists that it treasure the riches of our sacramental life, the deep roots of our spirituality, and the benefit of the historic ordering of laity, bishops, priests, and deacons.

The ability of these three expressions of renewal to make common cause was illustrated by the Three R's Conference that was held in Winter Park, Florida, in January 1986. Lay and ordained leaders representing these facets of renewal attended, and through fellowship, worship, and debate shared their concerns and sought a coordinated strategy. While this conference was indeed "a convergence of the saints," the participants failed to come away with a common agenda, and we do not believe it either possible or healthy for them to forge one.

As each of these strands has matured, not only have they been able to strengthen the Episcopal Church, but they have started nudging it in new directions. Church history suggests it takes about a generation for a renewing or revitalizing movement to begin making an impact. During the 1990s the renewal movements' concerns and agendas will come to the forefront. Yet despite their loyalty to the Church, renewal people have often been misunderstood and looked upon with suspicion by many in leadership.

Renewal Groups

Renewal has both parented and been parented by a variety of "submovements" that have further enhanced the Church's life. Many of these movements have grown in maturity and received a broader acceptance in many quarters, but it has taken a long time for the suspicion these activities engendered at the beginning to start fading. Today, however, there are few dioceses that have not benefited from Cursillo, Faith Alive!, Marriage Encounter, Happening, and the spread of the activities of Episcopal Renewal Ministries. Women and men whose faith has been brought alive by renewal have uncovered wonderful gifts of ministry. These have been put to use as members of Stephen Ministry teams, through evangelistic visitation of new-comers, or through selfless commitment to feeding the hungry, providing shelter to the homeless, or advocating systemic social change.

This has led renewal Christians to seek ordination in increasing numbers, and many are to be found in the student bodies of our seminaries. Some dioceses have found it necessary to establish creative, and at times restrictive, guidelines for those seeking ordination following a significant renewal experience. The enthusiastic faith of renewal Christians has not always been understood by seminary communities. The necessary marriage of academic theological discipline and vibrant spiritual experience is not easily achieved without pain, and sometimes mutual recrimination. Still, we anticipate that considerable numbers of renewal Christians will continue to heed this call to ordination.

Growing numbers of parishes during a rector search make use of the database of "renewed" priests developed by

Episcopal Renewal Ministries, in an effort to find a man or woman who is on their spiritual wavelength. Often these congregations are experiencing growth in numbers, giving, and extent of ministry.

Today there is a wide spectrum of independent agencies within the Episcopal Church, each with a clearly focused purpose. While the Anglican Fellowship of Prayer encourages the intercessory life of the Church, others focus on everything from youth ministry to evangelism and the conversion of the Jewish people. Voluntary mission societies like the South American Missionary Society are patterned after those found in other parts of the Anglican Communion. At Trinity Episcopal School for Ministry, renewal Episcopalians have played a part in the development of this seminary to train men and women for leadership in parishes and in this growing cross-section of independent ministries.

Most of these ministries will play an increasingly prominent part in the life of the Church in the future. Often launched as a result of the dream of a small group of visionaries, many are now neither unseasoned nor penniless. As their stars rise, we can probably expect to see them influencing the life of the Episcopal Church in new ways.

Bible reading is considered extremely important by most renewal Christians, and if purchasing habits are anything to go by, more Episcopalians are setting aside time for personal Bible study. Over the last few years, Forward Movement, which markets almost exclusively to Episcopalians, reports a steady increase in sales of their Bible reading resources. In addition, the Bible Reading Fellowship is expanding, and the Evangelical Education Society of Arlington, Virginia, has become the agent for daily Bible reading notes from the Bible Reading Fellowship of Britain. We see every reason to believe this trend will continue.

Renewal Agendas and the Wider Church

The findings of the 1989 Gallup survey, *The Spiritual Health of the Episcopal Church*, suggest a growing base of support for the likely agenda of renewal-oriented Episcopalians: evangelism, enriched spirituality, small groups, more opportunities for Bible study, and effective stewardship.

Presenting his report to the Presiding Bishop, George Gallup, Jr., writes, "In broad terms the picture of the Episcopal Church membership that emerges from this survey is of a church body that is substantially orthodox in its religious beliefs (with these beliefs in many cases grounded in life-changing religious experiences); committed to growth (both personal and institutional); open to change and new expressions of faith..."[1] Much of what Gallup describes is the fruit of the deepening influence of renewal in the life of the Church.

We believe it vitally important that this survey or something similar be repeated at regular intervals, no more than five years apart, in order that we can track the progress of the Episcopal Church. An accumulated corpus of information would enable Episcopalians at various levels of the Church's life to look for ways to meet emerging needs. An Episcopal research unit gathering, interpreting, and disseminating such data would certainly make trend-tracking and ministry planning less of a hit-or-miss business. Parishes and dioceses would benefit immensely from such an approach.

With their enthusiasm for sacrificial giving, renewal Christians have also played a significant part in the Episcopal Church's improving stewardship record. Not only do we have the largest per capita weekly giving of the traditional denominations, but by 1988 the Episcopal Church had the best figures for any denomination with more than one million members. Better stewardship has meant parishes and individuals are increasingly channeling funds in the direction of ministries that resonate with the goals of renewal Christians.

While renewal Christians have been "outsiders" for much of the last thirty years, a surprising number of overtly evangelical or charismatic bishops have been elected in dioceses all over the country. This is in addition to new bishops upon whom it might be difficult to pin a label, but who are strongly sympathetic to the aims of renewal. Although most media attention has been given to the possibility of women in the episcopate, we believe that, when the history of this period is written, the growing presence of renewal Christians in the episcopate will be yet another indication of the impact of renewal movements.

And this is a global phenomenon. Everywhere one looks throughout the Anglican Communion the ranks of the renewed are swelling.[2] Reading the statistics and monitoring their vitality, there is little doubt this is the predominant trend within worldwide Anglicanism, and it is conceivable that by the next century renewal Christianity will be on the verge of becoming the mainstream of the Episcopal Church. Those who ignore it do so at their own and the Church's peril. With each passing year it becomes more clear that if the Episcopal Church is to live up to its much-vaunted boast of toleration and comprehensiveness, the concerns and agenda of renewal people cannot be ignored by parishes, or by diocesan or General Conventions. As John Mulder writes,

> Fundamentalism has cast a long shadow over mainstream Protestantism, making these traditions distrustful, if not hostile, to the contemporary evangelicals in their midst....In the process, they have often missed the creative developments taking place in evangelical circles. Pluralism is desirable, it seems, only if it embraces more options from the left, not from the right.[3]

While church structures are unlikely to encourage fast progress to "center stage" by the forces of renewal, by sheer weight of numbers they are becoming increasingly difficult to stop. Renewal might begin small as a Faith Alive! weekend, a charismatic prayer and praise group, or a priest declaring a revitalizing spiritual experience from the pulpit. In some places it flowers under the ministry of a priest committed to faithful expository preaching from the Scriptures; in others it has a more sacramental flavor.

Despite the momentum of renewal, as an institution most of the Episcopal Church has yet to make serious attempts to understand the significance of this change of direction. One gets the impression in some circles that there has been an ostrich-like burying of heads in the sand. The Presiding Bishop speaks for many within the structures of the Church when he expresses anxiety about a resurgence of biblicism. He is right to be concerned about the aggressive, pharisaic edge that so often accompanies certain forms of enthusiasm, but within our tradition this renewed confidence in Scripture often has a more generous and tolerant face.

But It's Not All Plain Sailing

While we are certain that it will become dominant within the life of the Episcopal Church during the next decade or so, it will not be plain sailing for renewal Christianity as it moves to the center of the Church's life. On the way there are certain traps into which these movements could stumble.

First, there is the tendency for renewal Christianity to be fragmentary. Renewal is not a phalanx marching forward in lock-step, but an amalgam of organizations and streams of thought that have arisen at different times, in different places, to address different concerns while sharing certain doctrinal and spiritual presuppositions. Some renewal Christians express their faith with a charismatic exuberance that would startle the most enthusiastic Pentecostal preacher. Others find their faith refreshed and intensified in the quiet context of careful Bible study or retreat. Others still are brought alive through the Anglo-Catholic tradition's commitment to the daily Eucharist and the richness of an age-old spirituality.

The outcome of the Three R's Conference of 1986, when common yearnings were not able to produce either a shared agenda or a collective strategy, is evidence of the diversity in renewal. It is possible, in years to come, that renewal Christians could miss tremendous opportunities to advance because of their fragmentation. Ultimately, diversity might be their strength; during the next few years there are circumstances where it might be a weakness.

Second, certain of the movements that have accelerated the advance of renewal have reached a plateau. A number of dioceses, while admitting that Cursillo has transformed the lives of individuals and parishes, have observed that for the moment, at least, it appears to have peaked. It has yet to be seen whether this is a temporary breather in the midst of transformation or the beginning of a decline. Marriage Encounter is another renewal entity that appears to have lost some of its momentum during the last few years.

There may be good reasons for this. Perhaps the growing interest in spirituality and the interest in formation, which are the children of renewal, are leading us forward from Cursillo and its cousins to greater levels of spiritual maturity. One can only hope renewal does not fall into greater introspection, and ignore the fact that spiritual development is empowerment for mission and ministry in daily living.

Third, renewal Christians find it extremely easy to lose their positive outlook and focus on negative issues. It is less difficult to rail against sins of promiscuity, the inadequacy of inclusive language liturgies, or homosexuality than to do the theological and strategic work necessary to undertake holistic mission in the inner city or global evangelization, for example. Renewal Christianity also appears to have a strong aversion at times to using what Hercule Poirot so graciously calls, "the little grey cells"! The result is a tendency to lapse into an anti-intellectual Pharisaism. While this is a danger in every Christian tradition, it seems a special hazard in renewal circles.

A fourth point, which probably applies to renewal Christianity more particularly than the broader cross-section of Episcopalians, is the tendency toward "privatization of belief." It is our observation that renewal Christians are probably the most susceptible to extremes of individualized believing, despite a vocal commitment to the importance of community as expressed in the New Testament concept of the Body of Christ. A major problem of such individualized faith, based upon some definitive religious experience, is that it readily falls prey to cultural and theological relativism. This makes it vulnerable to phenomena like New Age religions.

While it is important that the Christian Church does not create artificial barriers over which we force people to jump if they want to be part of our community, there is a troubling tendency today to play down what is important and distinctive in Christianity—for example, to soft peddle the reality of sin in favor of good religious experiences and personal self-esteem. Too often, we want to make people feel good rather than enable them to nurture a relationship with God through Jesus Christ that leads to selfless discipleship. We perceive a tendency in the renewal movements to drift in this direction, unless they are rooted in a strong teaching tradition within the community of faith.

While the early stages of renewal are often accompanied by infuriating immaturities, most renewal Christians eventually grow beyond these and become ever more productive members of parishes and dioceses. On reading our description of the diversity of renewal, one of our correspondents, a parish priest from a southern diocese, wrote that the parish he serves "may well be a case study for the Church at large of the manifold blessings and occasional irritations of the renewal movement." His sentiments can probably be echoed a thousand times over, and that number is bound to multiply in the last decade of the century.

TRENDS TO WATCH

✚ The three distinct expressions of Episcopal renewal—charismatic, evangelical, and Anglo-Catholic—will cooperate increasingly, but will not move forward in lock-step.

✚ During the 1990s the concerns and agendas of the renewal movements will move to the forefront—not only here, but throughout the worldwide Anglican Communion, where these movements have become the majority.

✚ The renewal movements will provide an increasing proportion of all candidates for Holy Orders during the coming years.

✚ The network of independent, voluntary agencies the renewal movements have spawned will begin influencing the ministry of the Church—sometimes in unexpected ways.

✚ Renewal may lose some of its momentum due to the tendency to fragmentation, the plateauing of certain renewal submovements, and its tendency to focus on negative issues.

CHAPTER THREE

The Liberal Consensus
Begins to Erode

*I*f we are to grasp what the future holds in store, it is necessary to look backward and trace the path we have traveled on our way to this particular moment in time. History is the raw material from which the future is being sculpted.

The 1960s were watershed years for Episcopalians. Their churches had experienced unprecedented numerical growth without interruption ever since American soldiers had returned to civilian life following World War II. But in the 1960s, different agendas were thrust to the fore. Whether as a result or coincidentally, this accompanied a nationwide decline in religious involvement.

Forces that had been simmering in American culture for several decades, like the molten core of a volcano, erupted. Few realized quite how radically the face of America would be changed as a result of the cataclysm. As issues burst forth and demanded attention, the Christian conscience of the churches sought to address them. The resulting rift that opened up between those who believed the primary response to the Gospel should be social and political, and those who understood it in individualistic terms, still divides the Episcopal Church today. It is a smoldering conflict between people with strongly held convictions that occasionally becomes hot and angry, with a growing number of those at the center of the Church becoming ever more frustrated.

Like fault lines waiting for an earthquake, the potential for fragmentation had long been beneath the surface. It was not until the churches began thinking they had a major responsibility in righting social wrongs that sides coalesced and battle lines were drawn. In a few short years, an unpleasant, confusing, and sometimes bitter polarization had taken place. In this way the Church reflected the division of the wider society and culture.

"Liberal" versus "Conservative"

We ourselves confess that we often fall into the temptation to dismiss those with whom we disagree by presumptuously, and often inaccurately, labeling them. This leads to the discarding not only of the individual or group, but also of the integrity with which they hold their position. The labels that so readily fall from our lips are "liberal" and "conservative," both of which have become loaded words. Indeed, our own views and debate lead us to conclude that Episcopalians can very easily be liberal in certain areas and very conservative in other areas. As Walter Dennis, the Suffragan Bishop of New York, concludes, it would be foolish to lock up either conservatives or liberals in a box. He points out, "No liberal favors every proposed reform or everything labelled 'progress.' No conservative resists every change. Measuring either definition against individuals will inevitably produce contradictions."[1]

There are gradations of opinion on a liberal-conservative continuum in this and every church. There is little to be gained from labeling one another, because few groups or individuals are to be found in exactly the same spot on that continuum for every theological, social, political, ethical, and ecclesiological opinion. One of the great tragedies is that we have fallen into the trap set by our own labeling, and have grossly misrepresented the views of those with whom we disagree in the life of this very comprehensive Christian community. To help us in our observation of the movements within the recent past of our Church, and the trends that are shaping its future, we are using the following broad definitions, although recognizing that behind each of them is a far greater complexity of views than we have space to explore in this short book.

With the help of Bishop Dennis, we have drawn up the following broad definition of what it means to be a liberal:

> Liberals tend to approach reform as a response to the progressive revelation of God's will or intent. Not being restricted to the literal meaning, they argue that the Holy Scriptures and Word of God were written by God-inspired human beings who nonetheless lived at a distant time in a given locale; they must be interpreted by the church in light of events and interventions that could not be even dimly foreseen.[2]

The conservative understanding of biblical authority is rather different, being demonstrated here by the comments of Terence Kelshaw, Bishop of the Rio Grande: "Scripture is not subject to reason in the sense that one can *decide* upon scripture and accept or reject it at will. Reason *evaluates* the evidence and helps us to tie in the received tradition. Reason gives us courage to apply scripture rather than replace it. Reason helps us work out the ways in which scripture shapes us for service in the Kingdom of God....True faith will submit to scripture and its demands."[3]

Most Episcopalians who have given any thought to this topic will find themselves somewhere on the continuum between these two positions. As you read this chapter, whenever the terms "liberal" and "conservative" are used we hope that you will bear with our oversimplification of these complexities.

While we have pointed out that there are gradations of opinion on this liberal-conservative continuum, the painful truth is that two competing factions have faced off ever since the General Convention Special Program in Seattle in 1967. This was an attempt to respond to the bitter violence that had erupted in black ghettos throughout America, and the Special Program earmarked funds to address the problems in society those disturbances highlighted. Controversial grants were made, and a Special Convention was called in 1969 at the campus of Notre Dame University to debate widening the Church's range of participation. This was also the first General Convention at which women, ethnic minorities, and young people were present in significant numbers.[4]

Meanwhile, in addition to this challenge to institutional and societal evil, the Church was struggling to come to terms with radically changing patterns of personal behavior. "During the 1960's, a sharp liberalization of attitudes...took place on a wide variety of life-style issues ranging from divorce and premarital sexuality to political and economic orientations," writes Robert Wuthnow.[5] In *The Restructuring of American Religion*, he demonstrates that a parallel degree of liberalization affected every mainline religious tradition— Protestant, Catholic, and Jewish.

In addition, a theological consensus was emerging from most of our seminaries that both encouraged and affirmed the actions taken by the political and social left. In the 1950s, American churches sought to focus on issues of individual morality and family concerns; this was now pushed into the background and an agenda was adopted that sought to confront social ills and systemic injustice. Seminaries started abandoning the classic curricula of theological education. In their place came less structured offerings shaped by new methodologies being explored.

In this period, the development of Clinical Pastoral Education (CPE) had been encouraged by Episcopal seminaries, to enable seminarians to uncover their own personal identity and better integrate theology and the life sciences.[6] While we think highly of CPE and affirm the positive role it plays in forming the life of the emerging priest, in those extraordinary and critical times, the traditional understanding of ministry was replaced in the minds of many with a more therapeutic model. CPE seemed to encourage the assumption that the whole cross-section of human problems could be solved by programs, human movements, political action, and the remolding of people's minds.

The Dominance of the Liberal Agenda

All this provided the perfect environment for the ascendancy of a more liberal agenda in the Episcopal Church after 1965, and it seemed to carry everything before it, not only among Episcopalians, but in all the major Protestant denominations. Episcopalians of a more liberal bent who rose to prominence in the twenty-five years following World War II were often the exciting visionaries of our Church. Those on the more conservative end of the spectrum seemed slow-moving and out of touch with the events and presuppositions shaping the age, their consciences dulled to the injustices deeply rooted in American culture. This new generation of liberal Episcopalians became the leaders in the civil rights arena and the peace movement. They understood the spirit of the times and they attempted to address it in Christ's name.

They were sensitive to the changing role of women in American society, and played a prominent part in giving women their rightful place in the councils of the Church. It was mostly liberal Episcopalians who led the battle for the ordination of women, perhaps the issue that has most continued to strain the relationship between themselves and more traditional members of the Church.

Progressives in the life of the Episcopal Church list on their more recent agenda varying degrees of commitment to the pro-choice movement, gay and lesbian rights, the urban agenda, and justice issues in Central and South America. They continue to sensitize us to the issues raised by feminism, racism, and the shortcomings of the structures of American society.

Out of Touch

More liberal Episcopalians had a good understanding of these times, and the programs they developed appeared eminently relevant. Today, however, in many ways they have become the victims of their own successful reforms, and their agenda often now lacks that initial dynamic. There is a sense that the secular culture, tempered by limited theological reflection, has become the shaper of their agenda. The words of the "Gloomy Dean" of St. Paul's Cathedral, London, W. R. Inge, might be relevant in these circumstances: "He who marries the spirit of this age is soon a widow."

As we observe the rapidly changing contemporary situation, the liberals seem to continue to approach causes and concerns in this decade in a manner more suited to the 1960s. This has led some to question whether they are in touch with a very different sort of nation and world.

We do not wish to imply in any way that church and society between them have solved the problems of racial and sexual equality, for patently they have not and Christians need to say so. Neither can we stop worrying about threats to world peace and the effects of domestic poverty. But the conscience of America in the 1990s has a different agenda, and those at the more liberal end of the spectrum have yet to accept this reality. Furthermore, methodologies that may have righted wrongs in the past are far less likely to bring about positive change today.

The concerns of many of our people today focus on issues that personally impact their lives. They are anxious about the crisis in the American family and related issues like the provision of good health care for all citizens, the vanquishing of AIDS, and the ending of chemical dependency and substance abuse. This is not to mention the disintegration of the family by divorce and the resulting anguish to adults and children alike.

There is now a strong desire to protect our environment, and anxieties have arisen concerning foreign investment in the USA, the perceived global decline of this nation, and the struggle to find a just and moral way to deal with the abortion issue. This is closely coupled in the lives of many Christians to their search to live a ethical life in the midst of a seemingly hedonistic society.[7]

The 1960s produced a violent reaction against the ordered suburban world the G.I. generation had so carefully constructed. That decade also responded to internal turmoil at home, heightened by an unpopular war in Southeast Asia. Behind the issues of the present decade is a spiritual hunger and a yearning for strong and lasting relationships. Perhaps the liberal wing of the Church has not fully grasped the significance of this changing mood.

The relaxing of sexual restraint and three decades of growing divorce statistics have left a generation of shell-shocked children, and we have only begun to understand the long-term effects. This is the social environment in which today's Church is seeking to live out its witness. How we handle new family configurations, and respond to the damage done by the break-up of old ones, must be one of today's most pressing anxieties for Christians of all theological leanings, and society as a whole.

The discontent of the majority with the radicals' sexual agenda, especially the debate surrounding the legitimate parameters for homosexuals within the Church, is triggering the rejection of the wider agenda of the left because of strong disagreement with their stance on sexuality. We have talked to many lay men and women throughout the country for whom the sexual agenda of a liberal minority has become the symbol of a theological decadence that has sold out to a hostile secular culture.

We believe that human sexuality will continue to be a major point of contention throughout the 1990s. The 1991 General Convention's decision to refer issues of human sexuality back to the parish, diocesan, and provincial levels will further fuel this divisive debate. It has already been greeted by a simmering anger that will be much more difficult to satisfy than the discomfort prior to Phoenix.

Diminishing Returns

We do not wish to minimize the many significant achievements of the liberal tradition within the Episcopal Church, and the major role it has played in heightening a broader range of sensitivities. But today the style and content of their agenda appears to be losing the respect of a growing proportion of our membership. Liberals often claim that their stances are unpopular because they are "prophetic." There are occasions when such prophecy rings true, but there are many other occasions when such forthrightness has yet to prove itself. Such claims ring increasingly hollow because the causes being championed seem so far from traditional interpretations of scriptural values.

Writing in late 1990, Bishop Walter Dennis made a series of gloomy predictions about the future of liberalism and radical values in the Episcopal Church. Toward the end of that article he muses whether his pessimistic prognostications from a liberal standpoint do not make him "the Medical Examiner pronouncing the liberal agenda dead."[8] Unless something very unexpected happens, we have a feeling he might be. His words hint at the discouragement of much of the liberal wing of the Episcopal Church is as it views the future.

This tradition in the Church seems to be wandering off track. The Broad Church school within Anglicanism, of which modern liberals are the heirs, was marked by tolerance and generosity. Both within and beyond Anglicanism, too often these qualities are missing today. Their partiality and "illiberality" makes it difficult for them to embrace comprehensiveness and pluralism if it is to the right, rather than to the left, of themselves. Many find it extremely difficult to handle graciously positions that are politically or spiritually outside their own points of reference. This merely heightens the tension between left and right in the life of the Church.

Past Glories Do Not Translate into 1990s Successes

In the past, liberals were the social conscience at the heart of the Church and for this we must be grateful. Today the enthusiasts among them have pushed issues that are relegating them to the irrelevant fringe of Church life. They have left in their wake many, among both the clergy and the laity, who have liberal sympathies and liberal social agendas, but who find themselves baffled by the causes now being championed. Within the Church's organizational structures today they seem determined to hold onto the power bases acquired in the past two decades of preeminence. This sets the scene for an increasingly vitriolic clash with the growing conservative lobbies.

Liberal Christians have always been much more willing than others to believe the political process works. They are skilled politicians and understand the maneuvering of the conventions and councils of the Church, so that often in the past they have been able to get things done their way. Their success peaked at the 1976 General Convention in Minneapolis. On that occasion, both the revised Prayer Book and the ordination of women to the priesthood were passed. Successive conventions have greeted their agenda with less enthusiasm. Despite their skills in building coalitions and managing business as it goes through committees and debates, changing times and the erosion of support make their task an increasingly uphill battle.

While liberal voices are still insistent, during the 1980s they began losing their power to transform agendas of the Episcopal Church. As aggressively as they still express their opinions and champion causes, they are often on the defensive. The 1990s will see the coalescing of more conservative forces. These will not only alter the direction the Episcopal Church takes, but will likely rescind or modify certain facets of Church life that prevailed during the liberal heyday. During the next ten years we anticipate a continuation of the trend toward electing more conservative candidates as deputies at General Convention. It appears, for example, that Episcopalians United and their allies will mount a campaign to increase conservative representation among deputies at the 1994 General Convention in Indianapolis. This in turn may mean that items at the national level that are part of the liberal agenda, but are not now in place, could very well be removed from serious consideration in the future.

While the loosening of liberal influence in the Church will continue apace in the 1990s, it will be neither steady nor inexorable. As Episcopalians attempt to grasp what it means to be "comprehensive," in the best sense of that word, we can expect plenty of fireworks. We foresee the years ahead being difficult ones for those at the more liberal end of the Episcopal Church's theological and social continuum. While they will continue to be a force to be reckoned with, with each passing year we expect to see their influence waning, although it is unlikely ever to die away.

TRENDS TO WATCH

✚ Liberal Episcopalians will continue to champion a cross-section of causes in the areas of peace, justice, privacy, and human sexuality, thus intensifying polarization within the church.

✚ Conservative forces will coalesce to challenge the liberal wing of the Church, becoming increasingly well-organized and financed.

✚ All Episcopalians will be struggling to come to terms with the changing agenda society is thrusting before us.

✚ Sexuality issues will continue to inflame the tension between liberal and conservative wings of the Church.

CHAPTER FOUR

A Groundswell toward Creedal Orthodoxy

Whether it is deserved or not, the Episcopal Church's image has been that of a trailblazer and trend-setter during the past generation. The Roman Catholic ecumenical observer at the 70th General Convention in Phoenix, Arizona, said he considers the House of Bishops the Green Berets of the Church! This carefully cultivated stance has been further enhanced by the more "colorful" actions and pronouncements of some of our more media-savvy bishops and theological educators.

In recent years, the Episcopal Church has given the impression it is more fascinated with modern ideas shaped by the prevailing culture than with exploring the implications for today of the ancient formularies of the faith. This had made that segment of the Church's leadership that is theologically orthodox appear dull and unexciting. In addition, these prominent Episcopalians have not sought the publicity of the secular media like their more flamboyant counterparts; very often they have shied away from it. It has been the James Pikes, Paul Moores, and Jack Spongs who have set the agenda and been able to command media attention. Because of such exposure, while the media has ignored or been unaware of the voices of theological orthodoxy, the

37

watching world can be forgiven for believing that the views expressed by these men and women are those of the Episcopal Church at large. There is little doubt that the press continues to give the impression that their star is in the ascendancy.

This is far from the case, for the appeal of traditional Christianity appears to be on the rise. During coming years we expect our Church to present an increasingly orthodox theological profile. We agree with Bishop Walter Dennis, a self-proclaimed liberal, when he says that "the 1990's will see less theological speculation of the type put forward by James Pike, J.A.T. Robinson, and the 'Death of God' theologians."[1]

Probably one of the greatest surprises of the 1989 Gallup survey were the uniformly traditional beliefs held by the majority of those interviewed. The survey revealed that a huge bulk of lay Episcopalians are more orthodox in their theology than might have been expected. While there is incontrovertible evidence that the American people in general are fairly conservative in their religious views, one would not have been surprised to find in a highly educated denomination like the Episcopal Church, which until recently had been one of the shapers and arbiters of American attitudes and beliefs, signs of bucking this trend. This does not appear to be the case.

The Gallup poll demonstrated that at the grass roots there is a distrust of "ground-breaking" religious explorations. Whether educated in theology or not, Episcopalians are not comfortable with an agenda that appears to be set by modernity rather than by "the teaching...of the apostles." They have few arguments with the affirmations of the creeds and Holy Scripture, even if they are often unwilling to apply such demands to daily living.

Highly committed Episcopal Christians, as well as those whose faith is less wholehearted, are more likely to affirm historical, traditional, and orthodox tenets of the faith than adhere to the opinions of our more radical spokesmen and spokeswomen. Not always able to put their finger on what they think is wrong, Episcopalians are often uncomfortable with pronouncements made in the Church's name that they consider unrepresentative of the majority.

Either Episcopalians have grown weary of new theological fads and fashions, or more likely, they were never particularly excited or stimulated by religious pioneering in the first place. With only one set of Gallup statistics on the Episcopal Church to consult, we lack points of comparison to tell us whether this is a recent change of opinion or a deep undercurrent that has been there for years.

Like other mainline traditions, until World War II the Episcopal Church was a major player in forming American opinion and shaping the culture. Since then, as the culture has increasingly turned its back on even the residual standards set by Christianity, we have floundered and do not seem to know which criteria to use to challenge or affirm what is happening in society. Only now are we beginning to come to terms with the reality that this is a predominantly secular culture in which Christians are "resident aliens." During the coming decade we expect to see the Church beginning to work out the theological implications of this seismic shift in American cultural values, carving out a place for itself as a witness to, rather than an arbiter of, this secular society.

The Importance of Renewal

We believe renewal Christianity is playing a key role in accelerating this transition. Prepared to stand against the relativistic philosophies shaping society's beliefs and values, and more likely to affirm the historic Gospel as objectively true, it is highly likely that this will be the wing of the

Church in which we see consistent and holistic theologies developing. These Christians will increasingly nudge the Episcopal Church further back into the arms of creedal belief. This same trend can be seen within the wider Anglican Communion and it is no accident that the recently enthroned Archbishop of Canterbury, George L. Carey, is a product of the Anglican evangelical tradition.

This move back toward the theological center could be dismissed as a knee-jerk reaction, a return to the status quo, were it not so widespread and rooted in increasingly careful theological analysis and scholarship. Some might see it as a loss of nerve in the face of such a radically changing society, but we do not believe this to be the case. Traditional theological formulations are not just a product of the past, but shape both the present and the future. To some this might be interpreted as retreat, but large numbers of those on the road of orthodoxy have found the predominant liberal theologies of recent generations both anemic and powerless.

Among some Episcopalians there is also the perception that, taken to their logical conclusions, some of today's social and theological explorations in the area of morality threaten kinship ties and traditional family structures. For example, some of the conclusions being drawn by certain approaches to issues of sexual ethics have disturbed tens of thousands, many of whom cannot be considered adherents of either the political or the religious right. This has resulted in a level of distrust in the life of the church, the fear being that such wrestling inevitably accommodates the mores of an increasingly hedonistic culture. Is this a cul-de-sac from which escape is difficult?

The Stance of the Clergy

When comparing the clergy to the laity, it is apparent that the former are generally more liberal in their stances. As Archbishop George Carey has observed, "Many of us who have studied theology are more liberal than when we started out."[2] One only has to look at the divisions between clergy and laity in their choice of candidates in many episcopal elections to see this reality pointed up.

A significant proportion of the clergy in today's Church were formed in a liberal environment, in both their theology and their social analysis. Not only that, but there is strong evidence to suggest that the academic life, especially in our seminaries, attracts faculty of a more liberal ilk, thereby influencing the theological training future clergy receive.

A Presbyterian seminary professor has recently said, "Those of us trained in the universities and seminaries are socialized into a way of relating to the world that makes us unfit for working among the cultural right"—that is, the vast majority of Americans.[3] Tex Sample goes on to talk of "a great chasm" between professional church leaders and those in the pew. In all the mainline traditions the following critique is justified: "Theological faculties have, on the whole, moved from the center to the periphery of the thought-life of the Church."[4]

While we expect the clergy to continue to be theologically more liberal than the laity for the foreseeable future, there is every reason to believe this situation is being modified. The increasing attractiveness of creedal orthodoxy can be seen by the establishment of the Irenaeus Fellowship of Bishops in 1989, a forum for theological reflection. The Irenaeus *Statement of Beliefs and Purpose* has been signed by 74 members of the episcopate, 39 of whom have jurisdiction. Several other signatories had jurisdiction when they signed the *Statement*, but since then have retired from their dioceses. The Fellowship states its task is to uphold standards "based on the primacy of the Holy Scriptures, consistent with the historic traditions of the Church and interpreted by the best use of reason informed by the Holy Spirit." Recently, a group of priests in the Diocese of Michigan have sought to establish an Irenaeus Fellowship of Priests. Although it has yet to prove itself and get off the ground, properly organized and presented, this network could add priests as effectively as the movement that has gained ground among the bishops.

The response to the Irenaeus *Statement* by fellow members of the House of Bishops was somewhat larger than the initiators had expected. This alone seems to be a sign that the Church is reevaluating theological and social positions taken during the last generation.

At the 1990 meeting of the House of Bishops in Washington, D.C., furthermore, the episcopate marginally "disassociated" itself from the Bishop of Newark for ordaining a practicing homosexual to the priesthood. On that occasion, it was the younger and recently consecrated bishops who were most willing to provide the censure. That in itself might suggest that the House of Bishops is moving toward a more central position.

Another sign of the changing times is the creation of "Scholarly Engagement with Anglican Doctrine" (SEAD), which has a rapidly expanding membership whose purpose is to provide fellowship and nurture for scholars, pastors, and parishioners. Its goal is to reinfuse the Church with the fruits of a dynamic orthodoxy. The group describes itself as being "accountable to the tradition of classical Christian orthodoxy and to classical Anglican resources from which that tradition has been developed, and within which it is sustained." Focused around certain members of the faculty at Virginia Theological Seminary, SEAD could well start bringing to theological education an academic discipline rooted in creedal orthodoxy, rather than in the social ethics and psychology that have been shaping clergy since the 1960s. We believe the pendulum in seminaries is already swinging back both to a more biblical grounding and to a reemphasis upon spiritual formation that will be increasingly determinative in the coming years.

Creedal Christianity and Theological Education

While it is still a relatively young institution, Trinity Episcopal School for Ministry in Ambridge, Pennsylvania, founded in 1975 and fully accredited by the Association of Theological Schools ten years later, is playing an increasingly important role in the resurgence of creedal Christianity. Recognizing that other Episcopal seminaries have not always been rooted in the historic creeds, its presence has given a center of focus to that evangelical stream within the Episcopal Church that is so significant elsewhere in Anglicanism, yet poorly represented in the American Church.

Initially, Trinity was viewed as a "protest seminary," and most bishops in the Church were unwilling, and sometimes militantly opposed, to sending seminarians there. However, in recent years it has displayed increasing academic maturity, and the arrival as dean and president of William C. Frey, former Bishop of Colorado and a much-respected member of the House of Bishops, has modified the bishops' opinions somewhat. We expect Trinity will continue to be an important ingredient in the necessary theological education mix of the Episcopal Church.

Either because bishops continue to be apprehensive about Trinity, or for other reasons, increasing numbers of seminarians who have come from a renewal background are receiving their theological education at the more established seminaries. While they often find their views coming under pressure from certain professors, as we have indicated elsewhere, increasing numbers are maintaining their more orthodox theological orientation. During the 1990s we hope that students and faculty will develop mutual respect for the differing insights they bring to the theological task.

Since Trinity has been established, we have seen Virginia Theological Seminary hire several faculty whose theological bias is more creedal. Recently Berkeley at Yale seemed to be making a decisive move toward the center when it appointed as dean Philip Turner, formerly Professor of Christian Ethics at the General Theological Seminary in New York. Dr. Turner has been a leading figure in the conservative theological renaissance. He has been particularly forceful in providing theological and ethical undergirding for orthodox Christianity as it confronts the sexual chaos of today's society. If Berkeley at Yale is repositioning itself by this appointment, then creedal Christians are clearly poised to challenge what has been the dominant style of theological education in Episcopal seminaries during the 1990s.

However, even as we write, the future of Nashotah House, the bastion of catholic orthodoxy in the Episcopal Church, is in question. Caught between the Episcopal Synod of America and Anglo-Catholics who hold a more moderate position on the ordination of women, this once great seminary faces uncertainty. Should the school be unable to continue forming persons for Holy Orders, it will mean one less option for creedal Christians to receive theological education in the Episcopal Church. In the 1991-1992 academic year a radically reduced student body remained, many others having transferred to other schools throughout the country.

Not long ago we were talking to a priest from the West Coast. She told of a conversation with a seminary professor who, after exploring any number of trendy avenues over the years, is now moving back toward what our informant described as "a centrist orthodoxy." We expect others to tread this path as it becomes more obvious that the radical direction of theological reflection is not the only "staff of life" for the Episcopal Church. Although it will require significant retooling of our educational structures, both for the training of clergy and the equipping of the laity for ministry, those who overlook this move toward the center are likely to find themselves increasingly isolated during the next generation.

Renewal, Creedalism, and the Extremes

Renewal, which is self-consciously conservative in its theological bias, is likely to continue sharpening the theological perceptions of a growing number of Episcopalians. The antennae of renewal Christians will be tuned for ideas coming from Episcopal leaders that do not correspond with the substance of the faith, as spelled out in the ancient creedal formularies, the Scriptures, and the Book of Common Prayer. While we do not expect to see heresy-hunting of the variety that has marred the life of some Protestant denominations, we expect the threshold of tolerance for unusual, and sometimes outrageous, theological ideas to drop during the next ten years. This will be reflected by conflict at every level of Church life from the General Convention to parish vestries.

However, Episcopalians in general are not happy with extremes. Renewal movements will continue to have an impact on the life of the Church, but they are maturing. This growing orthodoxy is less likely to express itself in either the "lace and cotta" ceremonial of traditional Anglo-Catholicism or the emotional intensity present in some less contained varieties of charismatic worship.

This move toward the center might seem a refreshing change to many conservative Episcopalians who have despaired over the direction the Church has taken. However, we must be vigilant not to sacrifice the generosity embedded in Anglican principles. We must encourage a spirit of inquiry and a willingness to listen to and engage in dialogue with those with whom we disagree. It is vital for the health of the Church that we be able to beg to differ with one another, while continuing to pray together and remain in Christian fellowship. Such tolerance will be truly tested as the Church attempts to come to terms with the yet unresolved issues from the Phoenix General Convention.

At this point in the movement toward creedalism, we caution the Church against blocking honest theological investigation in its eagerness to be orthodox. Orthodox believing should honor the intellect while at the same time defend the substance of the faith. In most parts of the Episcopal Church there is little evidence of a witchhunt for liberal positions, yet the danger is always lurking in the background. With this caveat, we have an extremely attractive calling card for thoughtful, believing people seeking a spiritual home. This could be very important to the future well-being and growth of the Episcopal Church.

T R E N D S T O W A T C H

✚ We will see a deepening alienation of the Christian churches from the prevailing culture.

✚ Renewal movements will have an increasing influence on theological education and Christian belief within the Episcopal Church.

✚ There will be a decline in the attractiveness of "theological speculation" that has marked much of our recent public debate and discussion in the Episcopal Church.

✚ The rise to prominence of "dynamic orthodoxy" among Episcopal scholars will continue, with increased recognition of the importance of this orthodoxy by the seminaries.

✚ A dilemma will persist for Anglo-Catholic Episcopalians, which presently is reflected in the battle for control of Nashotah House.

CHAPTER FIVE

The Mushrooming of Spirituality and Formation Movements

*A*s we enter the 1990s, Episcopalians of all backgrounds and theological stances are exploring with increased vigor the spiritual roots of their faith. They are eagerly seeking ways of living and praying to bring themselves into a closer, deeper relationship with God. We are not alone in this venture. It is a trend influencing all mainline churches; however, we do not think it is an accident that the ecumenical journal devoted to spiritual development, *Weavings*, is edited by an Episcopalian.

Beyond the Superficial

The hunger for spirituality has many roots. On the one hand, it may be a reaction against the superficiality of our age and the empty materialism of the Church's suburban captivity. On the other, it might be that those who endorsed the social agenda of the 1960s and 1970s are finding it no longer meets the deep longings of their hearts and souls. One pollster and observer of American Christianity writes,

> Research...shows that pastors are especially concerned about the health of the Christian Body in America. Just one out of three believes that the Church is having a positive impact on souls and society. Two thirds say that the superficiality of people's faith is a very serious problem.[1]

Furthermore, perhaps we are seeing the inevitable maturation of the development that began with the charismatic renewal thirty years ago. Except for those who confuse childlike expressions of renewal for the working of the Holy Spirit, "the babes in the faith," a vast majority of those who come into a life-changing experience of God want to move on and grow up. Therefore, it is inevitable they will look for the nourishment they require in rich traditions of Catholic and Protestant spirituality to which Anglicanism is the heir.

The Prayer Book—A Resource

The search for nourishment in our tradition has been encouraged and enhanced by the 1979 Book of Common Prayer, of which John Booty says, "The decade of the '80's has been one in which more and more people have discovered the riches of the new Prayer Book."[2] Packed with treasures from the past, this standard for worship has indeed whetted people's appetites for more of "the old disciplines." The utilization of the Baptismal Covenant as a basis for many facets of believing, from development of a catechumenal process to a personal source of meditation, is but one example of the use of one of the newer spiritual resources available to us in the Prayer Book.

A three-year lectionary series now guides us to encounter Christ in the Christian year, helping us understand (with biblical "jewels" for our spiritual development) how we are to live out our resurrection faith in our daily lives. In all, it is a treasure house of materials for our reflection and growth.

Perhaps the time has come to develop this lectionary material further to include other themes, enabling reading and reflection upon an even more comprehensive collection of the Scriptures, even if it means moving from a three- to a five-, or even a seven-year cycle. Such a wealth of biblical material would provide richer food for thought and would be a fuller source upon which to draw in our spiritual development. Maybe the first move in this direction was signaled by the Phoenix General Convention's instruction to the Standing Liturgical Commission to investigate the possible usage in the Episcopal Church of the more comprehensive daily lectionary now in use in the Church of England.

The last decade has seen a significant increase in the number of women and men seeking spiritual counsel, going on retreat, developing their relationship with God through journaling, receiving advanced training on becoming spiritual guides, and reading the great classics of the faith. Publishers have responded to this thirst by producing modern books addressing this need, as well as reprinting the ancients from whose riches we continue to learn.

Furthermore, while Clinical Pastoral Education and the insights gained from a thorough understanding of oneself still figure highly among clergy, priests appear to be moving away from such a heavy dependence upon the therapeutic model as they exercise pastoral care, now realizing how much that ministry needs to be anchored in a strong spiritual life. This could be a source of considerable spiritual advance in coming years.

The Resurgence of Interest in the Religious Life

New religious orders are appearing in the Church, along with the renewal of some of the older, more established communities. In addition, there are now opportunities for married people to be attached to a house or fellowship of religious, such as the communities to be found in Detroit, Michigan and Aliquippa, Pennsylvania.[3]

While these evangelical and charismatic orders add a new "flavor" to the religious life, there has been a significant growth among those associating themselves with our more traditional orders like the Franciscans; the Society of St. Margaret in Boston; the Society of St. John the Evangelist in Cambridge, Massachusetts; and the Benedictines in Three Rivers, Michigan. There is even a blossoming of new, traditional communities of religious, like the Order of Julian of Norwich in Waukesha, Wisconsin. This latter order is a contemplative community of both men and women under traditional vows that has expanded rapidly during its brief existence, adding considerable numbers of oblates. The rule of life mapped out for oblates is demanding, and the community expected no more than one new oblate per a year— but already fifty have joined the ranks.

There are also religious communities whose membership is aging and dwindling. Often their main concerns are survival and caring for the remnants of what once had been a vibrant fellowship. However, for each order passing away several new ones are springing from the fertile soil of the Episcopal Church. These groups are likely to be beacons for spiritual growth in the highly technological age into which we are moving.

But what is this spiritual formation after which people yearn?

Called, Empowered, Sent

The baptized, who have been called by God to be his instruments in the world, have a need first and foremost to be anchored in God's presence. They are called to be a people who are convinced they are spiritually empowered because they know Christ.

God calls us, gathers us, continually converts and forms us in the *ecclesia*. Then he sends us out "to be"—to be Christ in those places and circumstances into which he has placed us. As the Book of Common Prayer reminds us, "Every Christian is called to follow Jesus Christ, serving God the Father, through the power of the Holy Spirit."[4] All who are baptized are called to make Christ known.

Living out this faith, being people of reconciliation in a broken church and world—moving away from ourselves and toward God, as Walter Brueggemann continually reminds us in his writings—makes us those who sing praise, offer thanks, and give God the glory in the midst of our culture that would so often only sing of and to itself. Such acts of praise are "counter-cultural activity." "Being Christ" and giving God the glory will not be without its costs. For that reason our anchoring needs to be firmly in God's presence, so we may indeed know the one we proclaim and praise.

Speaking at a conference at Kanuga, Gordon Cosby of the interdenominational Church of the Savior in Washington, DC used the analogy of "the river" as a place where the followers of Christ need to be immersed and continually washed by God's presence. The issue with which most of us are wrestling is, "Do we trust the river?" Scripture assures us that the Holy Spirit will guide us into all truth, that God will give us his guidance—but do we live as though we believed this? Instead, we tend to hedge our bets. Intellectually we trust the river, the empowerment of God's presence, but we reserve for ourselves secular power and influence in case the river does not flow! The dominant struggle of our faith in western culture is summed up in whether we are prepared to trust the river alone.

Life in the Church is often focused on self-interest instead of following the example of Jesus Christ, which is to be vulnerable. We see this need to exercise control in parish life, in the life of our dioceses, and in the national church, and this often takes the form of withholding pledges, assessments, and our own participation.

As the baptized, we are called to be instruments of God's love, changed people who are anchored in Christ and empowered by God's presence so we can be Christ in the midst of the world. That means we need to pay as much attention to our spiritual well-being as we do to other aspects of our life. The signs are that there is an enormously energetic movement in the life of our Church to seek this anchoring in God's presence, and for that we can only give thanks. As we profess our faith in our daily place, anchored and empowered by God's presence, we are then impelled to pursue God's will.

When Things Go Wrong

However, things sometimes go wrong. When there is a crisis or a separation in our relationship with God, we can lose our moorings and our spiritual discipline is destroyed. This is as true for clergy as it is for laity. As we look at clergy in crisis, we find people no longer anchored in God's presence. This leaves them with a sense of hypocrisy and shame, and with little or no foundation upon which to base their lives. At the St. Barnabas Center near Milwaukee, Wisconsin, an ecumenical treatment facility balancing spiritual, psychological, and medical care for clergy and their families when in crisis, a significant lesson is that the spiritual life is always the first thing to go wrong. As a result, they find themselves lost and certainly easy prey for whatever disease or temptation may come their way.

Recognizing that God has called us to be his people, a growing number of Episcopalians now search for ways to be firmly anchored in God's presence. Being so anchored can convert us to radical commitment and the wholehearted desire to discern God's will in every aspect of our lives.

One pitfall, however, is that the hunger for God can lead us to concentrate only on the development of our interior life, with little or no manifestation of our faith in our actions. It is vitally important that the fruit of our spiritual lives find a demonstration in Christian service. Things go wrong when our focus is only upon our solely personal relationship to Christ, and little attention is given to how we can seek and serve the Lord in others.

The danger inherent in this exciting trend toward the greater formation of our spiritual lives is an escapism that can take us away from our call to be followers and servants of Christ in a fallen world. The development of our interior life is meant to enhance the living out of our discipleship.

Forming the Called in the 1990s

The yearning on the part of many Christians for a wholehearted commitment is in stark contrast to the "soft" and nominal approach to believing that reflects the emptiness of present day western culture. The commitment of many Christians to their faith is shallow, and part of the reason for our past ineffectiveness is that we have assumed Episcopalians had a greater understanding of the foundations of the faith than they did. We have shied away from challenging them to move to deeper commitment for fear that we would lose them altogether. As George Barna writes,

> We tend to think that everyone knows the basics....The research shows that while people may have some "head knowledge" related to the Faith, they have insufficient context to comprehend what the beliefs have to do with day to day reality....We cannot assume that when we urge people to pray, they know what that means....Even on matters of knowledge, the research indicates that while people may

use concepts such as "sin" and "the Trinity" in polite conversation, they have little idea how those concepts fit into a deeper spiritual perspective.[5]

As the church in China has emerged from decades of persecution, its numerical strength has surprised even the most knowledgeable observers in the West. A significant ingredient of this growth has been the Chinese Christians' instinctive understanding of the importance of a process of spiritual formation that leads believers to an unwavering commitment. Their full churches have led to a creative methodology. Worshipers are led out of church following the service by a line of "pushers," making space for the next congregation. They are met outside the building by mature Christians, who gather them into small groups for catechesis. Supportive prayer goes on in other groups as these newcomers are formed in the Christian faith.

As indicated by this Chinese experience, the proclamation of the Gospel in both word and deed is about changing people's lives radically. Such change is not just for the unbaptized (catechumens) but also for those who already belong to the Body of Christ. People at various stages of their journey in the Faith can be brought into a process of formation, be renewed, and become committed followers because of a fresh encounter with Christ. Responding to such an encounter, people have a renewed understanding of what it means to live out what they profess to believe—no matter what the consequences!

In response to this yearning for spiritual growth, several processes of formation have been developed within the Episcopal Church. The method is simple: people are gathered together, allowed to inquire, asking the questions they need answered to better understand Christian discipleship, especially as it manifests itself in the life of the Episcopal Church. Reflecting on Scripture and their personal experience of God, they begin a process of formation in Christ, which moves them forward to an intensive journey during the Lenten and Holy Week season, culminating in the Easter celebration. During the fifty days of Easter they take seriously their formation for ministry, looking at their God-given gifts and seeing what and where their ministry is to be in their world.

Twenty-five percent of the dioceses of the Episcopal Church are at various stages of this or a similar five-stage process. We expect to see a steady increase in the number of dioceses using this formation process during the 1990s. This attempt to meet the hunger for Christian formation is not unique to the Episcopal Church, but is to be found in the Roman Catholic Church, and more recently in the Evangelical Lutheran Church in America. We believe that the future life and ministry of the Episcopal Church will be immensely enriched by the way this process enables both new and "cradle" Episcopalians to be formed for the adventure of Christian discipleship.

One Episcopalian, Marcia Brooks of Christ Church, Whitefish Bay, Wisconsin, has this to say about it:

> The thing that struck me about "Journey in Faith" when at last I understood it, was that it made perfect sense. What could be more central to our lives as Christians than examining, exploring, then putting into action our very faith? I marvel at its simplicity....For me, two critical elements in the process are Scripture reflection and study, and the individual faith story, but it took some time to convince me of the value of the latter! As a Connecticut Yankee and a "cradle Episcopalian" a pleasant, academic discussing of biblical passages was all well and good, but I was more than reticent to share my faith story—I was terrified! Once I had done it, I realized how important an exercise it was. Rather than being a confession or a testimonial, it was simply a way to answer, "How did I get here, to this parish and to

this point in my life's spiritual journey?" Much to my surprise and relief, telling my story to another person was at once reassuring and liberating. I now view the faith story as a piece of "standard equipment" for Episcopalians that we should have tucked away and ready at all times.

We expect that such formational processes will enable people to encounter our Lord in their lives, and move them from a lack of enthusiasm for proclaiming the Gospel to a more inspired response and willingness to become conscious agents of the reign of God in their life. As the formation movement grows during the 1990s, Episcopal Christians will start to let people know that we are a Church that is faithful to what the Scriptures say of Jesus Christ and what is expected of us, his faithful followers.

In the past we have tended to rely, like other mainline churches, on the culture to form us as committed Christians. We almost assume that the culture around us is "Christian" enough to shape and produce Christian commitment and Christian living in our people. In the Episcopal Church we have topped off that exposure to "Christian culture" with a confirmation class. Now we are reaping the fruits of relying on such apathy and assumption, for we are now confronted with the obvious truth that this has not worked in the recent past, nor will it work in the future. It shouldn't be a surprise to any of us that being a good American citizen and having a few confirmation classes "under your belt" does not make a committed Christian. In fact, half of the adults who attend adult confirmation classes are no longer active in their parish three years later. Among junior high students who attend confirmation classes, only one in twelve remains active after three years.[6]

If we are to be serious about forming people for discipleship, if we mean to bring them "to see Christ," we need to be prepared to do it with thoroughness and not settle for the superficial. Nor should we settle for that which offers little opportunity for people to look seriously at their life and to look at God, and his place in their lives.

We are impressed with new opportunities to form our young children in the faith, as we find in the "Worship Center" approach to Christian education, pioneered by the Reformed Church in America and now being adapted in many Episcopal parishes. This approach enables the stories of the Bible to be joined with young children's experience of God and their reflections upon that encounter. Their response to God's action in their lives is given expression through art, music, and drama, all of which are channeled to be expressions of worship. This is certainly not a superficial approach to the formation of the young, but is a way to root them deeply in this vitally important aspect of the church's life as the worshiping community.

The Quiet Revolution

We expect to see this quiet revolution continue to grow at the grass-roots parish level throughout the remainder of this century. It will fulfill the yearnings of the baptized, both young and adult, to be formed for Christ's service, and will become a major theme of the Church's life in the coming decade. The positive results of such a trend will hardly begin to affect us during the remainder of this century, for it takes fifteen to twenty-five years for such a movement to realize its full potential.

TRENDS TO WATCH

✚ Throughout the 90s Episcopalians will continue to seek out spiritual direction and instruction in prayer and intercession.

✚ The Book of Common Prayer and the three-year lectionary will be increasingly important as resources for spirituality.

✚ We will see further development of and experimentation with the religious life; healthy communities will attract adherents.

✚ Improved pastoral care will be available for those whose spirituality goes awry.

✚ Parish formation processes will pay more attention to the "basics" of the Christian faith and to the importance of the individual faith story.

CHAPTER SIX

The Liturgical Revolution Comes to an End

The last few decades have been marked by the most extraordinary liturgical ferment since the Protestant Reformation. It has been a period of significant and unsettling upheaval in the liturgical churches, not least the Episcopal Church. Almost independently of one another, Anglicans, Roman Catholics, and Lutherans pursued a process of liturgical revision, returning to the same ancient sources for the recovery of liturgical formularies. In each case it resulted in similar priorities and formats. In English-speaking Anglicanism around the world, we have returned to earlier orders of worship while using more contemporary language. Liturgical revision in the Roman Catholic Church has been even more revolutionary, moving from a Latin liturgy to one that is open-ended and extraordinarily flexible.

"We Love the New Book, Leave It Alone!"

In the Episcopal Church, with the exception of relatively small pockets of resistance, the liturgical revisions have been generally well-received, and the side effects of the revolution have for the most part passed. While there are still those who decry the departure of the 1928 Book of Common

Prayer, their ranks are dwindling. For the majority of Episcopalians, the 1979 Book of Common Prayer is now the
norm. Furthermore, teenagers' and young adults' experience of Episcopal worship is limited to the 1979 Prayer
Book, and a considerable number of those now being ordained have never known another standard of worship.

Although use of the 1982 Hymnal has been, for the most
part, optional, it has been surprisingly quick to be received
as the primary source of music in almost every Episcopal
parish. Likewise, there are those who grumble and refuse to
use it, but they are a small minority of the membership of
the Church. The 1982 Hymnal is frequently supplemented
in many places by the use of both official and unofficial contemporary forms of music and dearly loved hymns from the
Hymnal 1940.

A further sign that the revolution had achieved its ends, is
that in most parishes the Eucharist is now the main service
on Sunday. This was certainly the intent of the revisers as
they indicated in the introduction that "The Holy Eucharist,
the principal act of Christian worship on the Lord's Day and
other major Feasts, and Daily Morning and Evening Prayer,
as set forth in this Book, are the regular services appointed
for public worship in this Church."[1] In many dioceses, one
has to travel a great distance to find a congregation using
Morning Prayer as its primary Sunday service even once or
twice a month. The debate over the wisdom of such
sacramentality will continue into the foreseeable future, but
the prospect of the Episcopal Church backing away from its
decision to make the Eucharist the principal act of Christian
worship is, indeed, very slim.

Yet another facet of liturgical revision has been the opening of the liturgy to participation by members of each order
within the Church: lay persons, bishops, priests, and
deacons. Broadening such opportunities has enabled all the

members of the Church to fulfill functions proper to their respective orders, so that we can truly now say the entire Christian assembly participates in the liturgy of the Church.

Illustrative of the satisfaction with which the 1979 revision of the Prayer Book has been accepted by the overwhelming majority is the growing sentiment that further attempts to revise the liturgy in the near future will be met with strong resistance. People seem to be saying, "We have a new book, we've come to appreciate it, now stop playing around with it and let us enjoy it!"

There Are Continuing Issues...

The Gallup poll entitled *The Spiritual Health of the Episcopal Church*, surveying inclusive, non-sexist language in liturgy, reports that the "Don't Knows" and those who are openly hostile to such changes totaled 73% of those surveyed, thus indicating a large negative movement that would be difficult to overcome at the grass-roots level of the Church. Although most of the *Supplemental Liturgical Texts*, additional and inclusive language liturgies developed by the Standing Liturgical Commission and tested in many settings, were overwhelmingly accepted at the 1991 General Convention for use where the bishop of the diocese gives permission, we would be very surprised to see pressure to significantly revise the language of the Prayer Book in the near future.

However, beneath the issue of liturgical language is a critical theological exploration and debate that we expect to continue for many years to come. In a multicultural world, the western understanding of the nature of God, shaped as it is by the Greek and Jewish patterns of thought, is now being challenged. By the time the church is again ready to undertake a further major revision, the results of these deliberations will be more clearly discernible. We can expect the fruits of the present debate to alter the way we address God and describe humankind in our liturgical worship. This present set of circumstances will have a limited impact in the immediate future, but further down the road they will reach way beyond liturgical expression into our theological, educational, and missiological processes.[2]

There is now an ambivalence in the Church about liturgical revision. On the one hand, we have moved away from a static understanding of the liturgy, and are far more willing to accept the dynamic nature of ongoing liturgical review, which may result in further supplements for the Book of Common Prayer. On the other hand, since fewer and fewer voices are heard advocating an exclusive return to the 1928 Prayer Book, liturgical controversy becomes less and less the ditch in which clergy and interested laity are willing to die.

While recognizing that liturgical and linguistic experimentation and renewal are likely to continue in the future, we expect the 1979 Book of Common Prayer to remain the standard for Episcopal worship for at least the next two decades, although this will be enriched by a steady flow of resources made available for optional use.

"We Want Better Preaching"

While the majority are at ease with these changed patterns of worship in the Episcopal Church, new voices are raising serious issues concerning the quality of preaching, and the lack of Christian formation and education in the life of the Church.

The perception is that, since the 1960s, liturgical renewal has (for various reasons) discouraged the full-bodied sermon in favor of short homilies. In reality, the poor quality of preaching could well have led the laity not to encourage long, uninspiring, badly prepared addresses, which lack personal conviction and scriptural content. In the few places where excellent preaching has become the norm, the length of a sermon never invites criticism. Such preaching edifies parishioners, encouraging vibrant Christianity and active evangelism. Proclamation and exposition of the Word of God have always been, and will continue to be, a high priority for Anglicans when they worship God.

We expect that during the coming decade the quality of preaching is likely to become a major factor when parishes call new priests. Already, as we look at the priorities listed in parish profiles, the ability to be able to preach, and preach well, is very high on the agenda. The people of the Episcopal Church are telling us that the ministry of the Word during the last generation has left much to be desired, and that talks concerning issues and causes, ungrounded in the Gospel of Jesus Christ, have neither converted nor inspired them.

Now that liturgical anxieties are more settled, perhaps the Episcopal Church is in a position to direct more attention to preparing and upgrading the skills and abilities of those called to proclaim the Word to the People of God. There are already indications this trend toward improved preaching might be taking hold in the seminaries. That significant funding should recently have been made available for inter-seminary preaching contests for senior students is evidence this is a felt need that has to be addressed. In turn, this has stimulated seminaries to look at ways to improve the teaching of homiletics. We anticipate other strategies will be forthcoming to bring the standard of preaching up to the level demanded by the laity.

While the detrimental effects of preaching that is based on getting away with the least possible in terms of length, content, and preparation are still prevalent, in the coming decade we would expect the issue of the quality of preaching to be on the front burner of the Church's agenda. In the long term this will mean a slow but steady improvement in the quality of preaching.

Education, Formation, and Worship

Hand in hand with the demand for a higher level of preaching is an equally vocal concern to improve the quality of Christian education for both adults and children. As we will indicate in a later chapter, formation of adults in the life of the Church is leading to calls for the production of materials not only for younger members, but also for adults. Almost universally, parishes that flourish are the ones that provide fully rounded educational opportunities integrated into their Sunday morning program. Much material used is self-generated or borrows from other denominations, due to the unavailability of suitable educational materials in the Episcopal Church.

For nearly a generation, the Christian education materials known as the Colorado Series, *Living the Good News*, and based round the weekly lectionary readings, has been the only specifically Episcopal resource for multigenerational education. The recent introduction of the *Episcopal Children's Curriculum*, developed at the Virginia Theological Seminary in cooperation with Morehouse Publishing, is, we believe, a first attempt to address this void. The *Disciples of Christ in Community* program that grew from the ministry of John Stone Jenkins is yet another example of materials for Christian formation that take seriously the Baptismal Covenant.

We anticipate that during the next decade several curricula will emerge, having as their focus both Scripture reflection and worship, and the practical application of the Baptismal Covenant. We already observe that after only five years of implementation of the catechumenate, demands are already being heard for the development of similar materials to form our young people in their faith, and to continue building up the faith of adult Christians. Christian formation constructed around the catechumenal process has its focus in the relatively recently approved catechumenal liturgies found in the *Book of Occasional Services*, which demonstrates the vital link between the liturgy of the Church and the formation of the People of God. Some educators resist the development of such materials by the national church, but we believe that such resistance will encourage the production of curricula by independent entrepreneurial agencies of the Church.

As renewal Christians become increasingly influential, they will exert pressure on the wider Church to produce creative and inspiring materials for the formation of all generations represented in the life of the Church. And their voices are likely to be the most vocal demanding a higher quality of preaching from their pastors, thus challenging the present homiletic malaise. Such preaching and education materials will, of necessity, have to be grounded in the Scriptures, be liturgically-based, and have practical application.

Liturgy and Community

Loneliness is an American plague, and "the Church is better poised than any other institution in America to respond to the rampant loneliness of the American people."[3] We find ourselves wondering whether good liturgy undertaken within the context of welcoming parishes will attempt to address this hunger for community during the 1990s. Christian formation based on small groups will inevitably have a considerable impact on such relationship building if the connection is made.

As we look ahead there is, by and large, a general satisfaction with the liturgical styles that have emerged from the past generation's revolution. However, there continues to be a frustrating concern for the quality of preaching and the lack of formative opportunities to grow in the faith through the Christian education programs offered by our parishes. In the decade ahead, it will be recognized with increasing urgency that both of these issues are of integral importance to the future health and welfare of the Episcopal Church, and we look forward to an infusion of resources and energy to enable the fulfillment of these goals. Education, preaching, and Christian formation must now move to the center of the stage.

TRENDS TO WATCH

✛ After years of liturgical upheaval, we are moving into a quieter period. It will not be free of controversy, but liturgy is unlikely to be the focus of dispute it has been in the past generation.

✛ Despite the authorization of supplemental texts there will be resistance to making changes in the Book of Common Prayer.

✛ The work now being done in the area of liturgical language and theology is likely to continue, but will not come into serious play until the next liturgical revision—probably in the early part of the next century.

✛ We will see great emphasis placed on improving preaching, teaching, and instruction in Christian formation in the next decade.

CHAPTER SEVEN

The Rising Profile of Women

The shift toward women as pastoral leaders on a par with men would appear to be irreversible at this stage, despite the continuing discomfort of those for whom an all-male priesthood is a non-negotiable element of historic catholicity. This acceptance of women in the ordained ministry of the Episcopal Church is borne out by the Gallup survey. Only 26% of those polled in our Church disapproved of the idea of female bishops, which suggests that a far smaller proportion dislikes the idea of female priests.[1]

These trends in ordained ministry are not isolated examples of the churches going their own way, but reflect the changing role of women in society around the world. In their book, *Megatrends 2000*, John Naisbitt and Patricia Aburdene Morrow point out that

> for the last two decades US women have taken two thirds of the millions of new jobs created in the Information Era, and will continue to do so well into the millennium....The tasks of business have changed and so has its work force. That is perhaps the main reason why the organizing principle of business has shifted from management to leadership, opening the doors to women.[2]

As the recent Lilly Endowment study looked at the changing shape of the Presbyterian Church (USA), the emerging picture of the role of women was similar.

> Women now constitute a major segment of the work force. An estimated 56% of women now work outside of their home, with roughly equal numbers of mothers and empty nesters holding down jobs. More importantly, women have caught the entrepreneurial spirit in a major way, now owning almost three out of every ten small businesses, and opening new businesses over five times more often than men.[3]

The indication is that women will continue to join the work force in increasing numbers. "By 2000 more than 60% of all working age females will be employed."[4]

Each year, as the Church grows in its experience of women in positions of ordained and lay leadership, it is becoming apparent that they bring important gifts to ministry that were missing when men dominated all positions of leadership in the Church. As the proportion of female priests increases it is inevitable that the pastoral role will significantly change. Some have pointed out the danger that the ordained ministry could be "feminized" to such an extent that it could be perceived to be almost exclusively a female profession. We do not believe this will happen, but ordained women are already forcing us to rethink fundamental aspects of pastoral ministry and church structures.

The Seminary Bubble

While the doors of most seminaries have been opened to full female participation, with the caliber of women entering often higher than that of their male counterparts, parishes have been slow to offer opportunity to ordained women with the openness they usually show to men of comparable ability.[5]

The Council for the Development of the Ministry has monitored this situation with the help of the Episcopal Women's Caucus, attempting to detect trends among women who had been ordained for ten years. During the first decade women were being deployed on only a slightly slower track than their male counterparts, but the indications were already emerging that parishes tended to be resistant to the concept of women as rectors or priests-in-charge of a parish. Granted, some female priests expressed premature frustration, as it does demand some experience to move into this kind of leadership position, but their frustrations are increasingly legitimate. Only a few parishes in most dioceses have reconciled themselves to calling a woman as their rector, even when deployment policies have been established to include women in the search process.

During the 1980s the worst fears that female priests had been verbalizing for some time were realized—no jobs, or limitations on job availability to women, usually as assistant clergy or "mission" priests. There has been an angry reaction among some women, a small minority of whom have turned their backs on the Church in despair.

However, in the early part of the 1990s we sense the tide might be turning. There seems to be a renewed openness to deploying female priests, perhaps because women in orders are no longer a threatening novelty. Search committees in certain larger parishes have sometimes insisted on women being candidates. It is conceivable that this "bubble" will be integrated into the life of the church, giving women equal opportunities and consideration on the basis of their gifts and experience.

At this point in time we can see a subsidiary debate developing around the issue of the increasing numbers of ordained women being trained by our seminaries, and the growing shortage of parishes and ministries who will make use of their considerable gifts and skills. We believe, however, that the 1990s will be the decade in which women who are clergy go to great lengths to demand their "place in the sun."

Revolution in the Episcopate

Nevertheless, despite these difficulties, women are reaching more deeply into the leadership of all the churches, and in this the Episcopal Church is no exception. The consecration of Bishop Barbara C. Harris may be said to stand at the end of a long historical development that affirms the ever-increasing role of women's leadership in the life of the Church. While the outcome of future episcopal elections is hard to assess, the likelihood of more women being elected bishop during the next ten years is high. Since the elevation of Bishop Harris to the episcopate, the Church in New Zealand has elected the first female diocesan bishop in our Communion. That this occurred elsewhere in the Anglican Communion emphasizes that the movement of women into all orders of ministry is a worldwide phenomenon. It is only a matter of time before a diocese in the Episcopal Church elects a woman to hold office as diocesan bishop.

This trend is certainly not welcomed by all members of the Episcopal Church, and whether the issue of women in ordained ministry will further divide the Church is still hard to predict. At this stage the intentions are not clear of those who are part of the Episcopal Synod of America, the primary body that bears the standard of opposition to the ordination of women in the Church. There are now loose links between those in the Church of England and elsewhere in the Anglican Communion who are opposed to the ordination of women, and this alliance will merit close observation in coming years.

The Archbishop of Canterbury's open championship of the ordination of women to the priesthood of the Church of England points to the inevitability of women entering the priesthood and eventually the episcopate of the our Communion's mother church in the not too distant future. This could coalesce the potential possibility of some form of "continuing Anglican Communion" coming into existence. From this perspective in time, it is hard to tell how large and deep such a schism in the Church would be.

These opponents base their position on the belief that such ordinations are not permissible because they contravene their interpretation and understanding of the principles of leadership to be found in the New Testament, and the historic traditions of the Church catholic. On the other hand, it has to be pointed out that there are substantial numbers of Episcopalians who hold an equally high view of the authority of Scripture, and affirm the validity and importance of women, ordained to leadership in the Church.

We believe the debate over the ordination of women will continue in the life of the Episcopal Church for the foreseeable future. It is our hope that we can be generous enough to hold together both opponents and proponents in this debate, as is envisaged in the canons of the Church.

Lay Women & Leadership

Together, female lay and ordained leaders will probably be catalysts calling us to put greater stress on community, informality, and nurture in the life of the Church. It is also surmised that a depth of women's leadership "will result in less emphasis on program and structure and more on nurture and human touch."[6]

Several people have observed that well over 50% of all vestry persons in the Episcopal Church are now women, who also make up a growing number of both junior and senior wardens. The highest position a lay person can hold in the Episcopal Church is now held by a woman, with the election of Pamela Chinnis as president of the House of Deputies of the General Convention in Phoenix in 1991. She is the first woman to hold this post. The great gifts women's leadership, both ordained and lay, brings to a Church that has been dominated by men for far too long are fresh ideas, different perspectives, and a wider range of leadership styles than had previously been acceptable.

We see leadership being exercised by lay women throughout the Church from presidents of provinces to a substantial participation on a wide variety of diocesan committees, as well as at the parish level. Credit for this rising profile and increased numbers of participants has to be given to a variety of sources, and various organizations and activities have prepared women for the leadership they now exercise:

✚ Diocesan schools for laity, offering courses in theology and the teachings of the Church.

✚ Education for Ministry (a program of the University of the South) and other continuing education opportunities, which offer deeper theological understanding and direction for ministry. Women have often pursued seminary courses just for the pleasure of deepening their theological knowledge.

✚ Leadership development offered by the Office of Women's Ministries at the Episcopal Church Center, and related to this, "Women of Vision," which provides opportunities for women to identify their gifts and enhance leadership at a parish, diocesan, and national level.

✚ The Episcopal Church Women in many dioceses now offer women a host of opportunities in the total ministry of the Church, rather than being restricted to traditional "women's work."

✚ Women have traditionally held leadership positions, sometimes professionally but most often as parish volunteers, in the area of Christian education. There is evidence that this is still the case but these roles are often radically changed. We find women on the creative, cutting edge of the Church's life. They have often been the impetus behind the Church taking Christian education and the formation of our youth and young adults with a new seriousness.

✚ Much of the most significant Bible study is done by small groups of women meeting regularly for study and prayer. Increasingly, these gatherings are the powerhouse for change and spiritual growth in congregations. It is often in such gatherings that women of all ages discover gifts for ministry and a vocation to a deeper commitment to Christian leadership.

✚ You don't have to look too far in most of our dioceses and parishes with large staffs and you will find lay women in key administrative jobs that in the past have been the prerogative of men, ordained and lay. Furthermore, many of our social services and outreach ministries are now led by women. In many places, this, too, is a major shift in what were once considered traditionally male roles.

All these build upon the foundations laid by generations of devout Christian women, without whose service and gifts the ministry of most parishes would have been paralyzed. The growing participation of women in leadership in the Church has begun an evolution in the way we make decisions. Their sensitivities have enabled the voices of a broader spectrum of people to be heard, and moved us away from authoritarian models of decision-making toward those based upon consensus.

Where Have All the Men Gone?

The changing role of women has precipitated a crisis among significant numbers of men, who have retreated from leadership in the life of the Church. Instead of withdrawal, it is our hope that men would respond to this extraordinarily radical trend that has reshaped the Church during the last generation, and that it would prompt them to take a new and revitalized role in the Church's life and ministry.

There is a noticeable and growing interest among men in many parishes to form support groups for men. In some places this has led them to begin exploring leadership processes for men similar to those developed for women. We expect that a growing number of parishes and dioceses will spawn small groups for men, lay and ordained, who will attempt to create such opportunities for their peers. Perhaps lessons will be learned from those leadership courses for women to which we have already referred. There is a definite need for men to continue to develop a sensitivity to the concerns being raised by women, while at the same time neither avoiding nor denying the issues of their own masculinity. The emerging "men's movement" in the wider society is, perhaps, a signal that men are ready to rethink their role. We hope that women will find acceptable ways to rejoin them in many Christian leadership roles.

The growth of women's leadership in both ordained and lay ministry has been impressive. It is a trend that is likely to continue for many years to come, but we still expect both the episcopate and the priesthood to remain predominantly male for at least the next generation. Despite this, we anticipate that the movement toward the full participation of women in the life of the Church will continue to grow.

TRENDS TO WATCH

✚ Despite the continuing discomfort of those who are convinced of the necessity of an all-male priesthood, the numbers and influence of ordained women will grow.

✚ The debate over the ordination of women will continue into the next century.

✚ A woman will be elected diocesan bishop in the Episcopal Church, although it is hard to predict exactly when.

✚ Women, lay and ordained, will encourage community and nurture in the life of the church, and are likely to change the decision-making process.

✚ The growing importance of women in the life of the church will stimulate men to alter their approach to and involvement in Christian faith and activities.

CHAPTER EIGHT

New Ministers for a New Millennium

W hen each of us was baptized, we were commissioned as ministers of Christ's Church to proclaim to the world "by word and example the Good News of God in Christ." We agreed to this commissioning "with God's help." Ignorance of our calling, confusion over its meaning, and broken promises have crippled the ministry of the Church, with the result that we have often been the People of God in name only—nominal Christians, in fact!

We have heaped an almost impossible load of expectations on the clergy, who themselves are in the midst of a crisis of identity. They lack clarity of role and do not understand the function of their particular order—bishops are just as confused as priests!

> It is far more difficult to be a pastor in the rapidly changing world of today than it was back in the 1950's.

> The most pervasive ministry frustration expressed by pastors is that they feel they bear the burden of ministry alone. Relatively few pastors feel as if they are part of a team of people working together to enhance the spiritual condition of the congregation and the world.[1]

Such confusion and frustration has detracted from effective ministry. Bombarded with a confusing array of expectations, neither the clergy nor the laity know what to expect of one another.

This confusion and the resulting paralysis have not gone unaddressed. The increased anxiety this situation has generated has resulted in groups and individuals throughout the Church attempting to find creative ways through the impasse. During the coming decade the fog will begin to lift and the practical implementation of new definitions will be explored with intensity. Like so many other changes, this is likely to cause much discomfort as old patterns of ministry become extinct and new ones emerge.

But the Church is beginning to retool....

Where's the Confusion?

We have turned bishops into administrators and priests into therapists, with the result that the building up of the People of God has been ignored. While accepting that this is a caricature of a more complex scenario, it describes the tangle we have got ourselves into. The time is long past to give the kind of attention, through study and reflection, to the ministry of bishops and priests that has been afforded the order of deacons in some dioceses during the last generation. This confusion is further compounded by the muddled and conflicting expectations that the laity lay upon their clergy.

This is not a dilemma restricted to the Episcopal Church. Christians of all theological persuasions, both Catholic and Protestant, are wrestling with this critical issue. In our own Church, the bishops are seeking a better understanding of their own ministry, the canons on ministry are being clarified, and everywhere understanding the total ministry of the baptized has become a high priority.

During the next decade the Church will step up its effort to unravel this confusion of roles. However, it will take a great deal longer for the Episcopal Church to reach a fresh vision and a reshaped ministry. The constant, rapid change of the world in which we live demands that reappraisal and revision will be permanently embedded in all future understandings of ministry. This in turn will stimulate new vision.

Out of all the work that is beginning, both within and beyond the Episcopal Church, a number of models for ministry are emerging. However, we expect it will be a good few years before any clear patterns become obvious. At the same time there are deep-rooted problems among the clergy that we will be forced to address during the remainder of this century. This is a full agenda.

Are the Clergy Backing into the Future?

In a speech to the Episcopal Church Foundation in 1991, Daniel Matthews, rector of Trinity Parish, Wall Street, said, "What concerns me most is that the Episcopal Church will back into the future rather than take deliberate action. I fear that we will be driven from one crisis to the next."

The corporate world has identified a series of early warning signs of organizational decline. We believe these are pertinent to the dilemma facing the Episcopal Church. Among them is to be found:

—Excess of personnel
—Tolerance of incompetence
—Disproportionate staff power
—The replacement of substance with form
—The scarcity of goals and decision-making
—The loss of effective communication
—Outdated organizational structure
—Cumbersome administrative procedures

This is an apt description of the tired machinery of the Episcopal Church, for which a major overhaul is long overdue.

The statistics emerging from one East Coast diocese verify these early warning signs. The diocese in question reached its highest recorded membership in 1960 (148,000 persons). Thirty years later it was reporting barely half that membership (75,000 persons) in an environment that has seen steady population growth throughout that period. At the same time nationally, in 1960 there were 7,500 Episcopal clergy, a roster that had doubled in number by 1990.[2] We believe these statistics are indicative of a deeper underlying malaise in the life of the Church that is begging for attention.

Meanwhile, we continue avoiding the implications of our folly. Bishops and dioceses continue to accept large numbers of postulants in the ordination process, while at the same time they are painfully aware of the declining number of full-time positions even in their own locality.

Closely related but often inadequately addressed is the high percentage of men and women who become candidates for the priesthood in middle age. Often struggling with mid-life transition, many of these would-be priests head off for seminary in search of the deeper meaning of life, while looking for the career satisfaction that to this point has eluded them. For many this follows closely on the heels of a personal crisis, or a dramatic renewal experience. It is unfortunate that some of these people bring unresolved problems with them when they enter seminary.

The career priest, able to give thirty to forty years to ordained ministry, is fast becoming the relic of a bygone age. Many of those entering the priesthood late do bring nurturing skills and insights from their previous life, but their presence leaves us with a limited number who can give themselves to the ministry of children, young people, and young families. We expect this is going to hinder our progress among baby boomers, subsequent generational groups, and their offspring.

If we are to be a Church that has as much appeal to the young as the older members of our community, we must give more thought to those who receive a vocation to ordained ministry at an early age. In some places we see a return to recruiting and accepting younger vocations. Already some bishops and dioceses are revamping their process toward ordination, indicating a need for generational balance and encouraging young men and women to offer themselves for service.

Not only do we believe this to be an exciting trend, but we are convinced it is most necessary. It would be wise for other dioceses to follow closely in the footsteps of those who are moving in this direction. The former dean of the Church Divinity School of the Pacific, William S. Pregnall, expresses the problem well: "The Episcopal Church is an aging Church....Therefore, if we are to have a Church at all in the future, we had better intentionally focus much of our energy on keeping those children who are born to Episcopal families...."[3]

Meanwhile, the presence of an older student body together, with women with families, has challenged seminaries to review their whole manner of operation. At a time of great stress upon the institution of the family, our system of theological education places the families of large numbers of our seminarians in jeopardy.

These are just a handful of the difficult questions concerning theological education with which the Church must wrestle in the years ahead.

Continuing Education

Today's adults will always be going to school. Continuing education is becoming part of the warp and woof of our careers, enabling us to remain proficient in our employment. Everyone from accountants to automobile mechanics is required to undertake significant blocks of continuing education in order to retain their certification. Should we expect less from clergy?

As we look round the Episcopal Church there are only a handful of dioceses with policies and programs that encourage or require clergy to remain current in both knowledge and skills. For the most part, it is left to the individual clergy person to plan and pursue his or her continuing education. It is our observation that even when time and funds are set aside for such enrichment, a significant proportion of the clergy fail to take advantage of something expected in many other fields.

In the Information Age in which we now find ourselves, updating of skills has become the norm and, as we have seen already, is required in many professional contexts. For the Church and its clergy to fail to adopt similar policies is suicidal. Not only will priests deprived of these opportunities for renewal and growth die on the vine, but their parishes will rob themselves of ordained leadership with vision to find the way forward and skills to plot an exciting course into the future.

"Leadership is the ability to read the signs of the times and point the way in times of change and crisis....Leaders establish the vision for the future and set the strategy for getting there," said Daniel Matthews in the speech mentioned earlier. While no amount of continuing education can eradicate incompetence, properly used it is capable of fertilizing the seeds of leadership many clergy possess, but which may lie dormant, waiting to be brought to life.

The Evangelical Lutheran Church in America requires its bishops to participate in a unit of continuing education on an annual basis. This is not only a fine example to their parish clergy, but is a model that might be imitated by the House of Bishops of the Episcopal Church.

Hope Waits in the Wings

It is fortunate that there are those who have dreams about the Church's future health as well as the ability to turn them into reality, especially as it applies to the full-time clergy of the Church. Substantial resources have already been allocated in certain quarters to research ways by which this deficiency might be addressed in supporting and developing the skills of our clergy during their working years. Parties already working in this area are various seminaries, the Episcopal Church Foundation through the Cornerstone Project, the Alban Institute, and certain dioceses.

Approaches are comprehensive in nature, dealing with every aspect of the clergy task, from entry into ordained life through programs to strengthen the ministry of bishops. The trend is toward developing a lifelong learning environment to support clergy in their work, and making provision to address crisis in the lives of clergy and their families whenever necessary.

Pastoral ministry requires a variety of skills, from the ability to care for the needs of their people and themselves, to the equipping and nourishing of the Christian community for ministry in an ever-changing world. Clergy also have specific individual skills that require identification and refinement, so that these might be used to enhance their wider ministry. We anticipate that such support resources and opportunities to upgrade these skills will also become more available to those who work as full-time lay ministers of the Church.

Because the laity recognize the need for competent and disciplined clerical leadership, we believe that as these programs begin to bear fruit in the lives of their pastors, they will elicit an increasingly generous response. Enabled in this manner, as the new century dawns, we could very well find ourselves on the way toward a quality of leadership that the Church has lacked in more recent years.

Mutual Ministry

If at a national and diocesan level we are moving from hierarchical models of organization to more democratic and participatory networks, in the parish local patterns of hierarchy are also under fire. While "traditional" pastors may do all they can to cling to their old authority, a shift is underway to a more scriptural model of the local church as an incarnation of the Body of Christ.

For a generation or more, clerical dominance has been slowly eroding, while there has been a tendency for certain priests avidly to hold onto their old status of "Father Knows Best." During the 1990s we expect to see broadening acceptance of the more organic model. This will challenge increasing numbers of clergy to reconsider the nature of their task, not only to be pastors, priests, and teachers, but also to nourish Christ's people and strengthen them to glorify God—in short, to build up the family of God.

Priests are called to equip the community of faith for their ministry in the world, not to see themselves as the provider of all ministry in the parish. (This stance may feed the ego, but it does not necessarily extend the reign of God.) Ordained women will certainly help us explore some of the more subtle implications of nurture and human touch that are implicit in this trend toward a changing model of ordained ministry.

In parishes where there is an almost total reliance on the priest, there is often an apprehensiveness on the part of the laity to become involved, leading to friction between priest and people. It is in such parishes that we find trouble, and that trouble is often focused on the way in which the priest exercises his or her ministry. Such friction can also be the result of a lack of understanding between clergy and lay leaders, which leads to inflexibility resulting in the inevitable failure to incorporate the laity into the total ministry of the parish.

Clergy need to learn to identify which tasks are appropriate to their gifts and office, and which to let go. It is often issues of status, or the perceived threat of losing authority, that leads clergy to be overly defensive. It is becoming increasingly apparent that the primary task of the priest should be to enable the whole People of God to exercise a fruitful ministry. This trend toward seeing the pastor as an enabler for ministry is not merely an Episcopal or even an American phenomenon; observers of worldwide Christianity suggest this is a movement with international and ecumenical dimensions. A college professor and international church consultant, James Engel, reporting on his experience with church leadership seminars in Asia and Africa, has said:

> The rise and growth of discipling/equipping is the biggest and most exciting thing happening. I sense it all over the world. I find the Lord has laid it on the hearts of pastors and church leaders wherever I go. This is a major shift, and I think it is a historic return...to a much more scriptural approach to the church.[4]

In the Episcopal Church today, the multiplication of small groups in parishes is a local reflection of this international trend toward discipling and equipping. For example, the African Bible study method is now being used in an increasing number of parishes, led by lay men and women, who have been equipped for such ministry by their clergy. They in turn are leading people to exercise discipleship in the world.

However, the institutional nature of our particular Church continues to resist this grass-roots inclusion of all God's people in the ministry of the Church. Such muddled thinking is reinforced by the inability of Episcopalians to understand properly the nature of either the ordained or the lay approach to ministry.

Such models of ministry, and continued improvement in the quality of the clergy and their working relationship with the laity, will move us toward excellence, for "churches which evoke a sense of quality will be more attractive than those that simply continue to perform their usual routine, oblivious to standards."[5] If we can get beyond the present paralysis and misunderstandings, it is our belief that exciting opportunities for mutual ministry and mission lie ahead for the People of God.

TRENDS TO WATCH

✠ The Church will experience a growing discomfort with old patterns of ministry. We expect to see the serious exploration of new options in the 1990s.

✠ The emphasis of clergy work in the coming years will be more on equipping the laity for ministry—the ministry of all the baptized—and this will begin to re-mold the curricula in our seminaries.

✠ The Church will acknowledge the need for lifelong in-service training for ordained persons and full-time lay workers.

✠ It will begin a review of the selection process of vocations for ordained ministry. We expect a process that has been loaded against the young in the last generation will start swinging more in their favor again.

✠ Other Christian traditions and denominations will be rethinking ministry as much as we will—and maybe more.

CHAPTER NINE

Outsiders Flock to the Episcopal Church

*I*t was late April, a warm early autumn evening in the Argentine city of Salta. We sat in a sidewalk cafe with a Canadian missionary priest drinking coffee, talking and watching the dusk fall over. Although thousands of miles from our respective homes, the topic of conversation was the Episcopal Church. The Canadian had been a lifelong observer of the American scene, and said how impressed he was by the loyalty of Episcopalians to their Church, compared to Anglicans elsewhere.

He was right. There is, perhaps, a stronger bond between Episcopalians and their Church than in other traditions. We have heard similar comments about Episcopal loyalty from Methodists, Lutherans, Roman Catholics, and Southern Baptists! Most of us revel in a "love-hate" relationship with the Episcopal Church. We see its warts and blemishes all too clearly, yet even while it infuriates us, we cherish it. We sometimes disagree with the pronouncements made by our leaders that make us angry, and we are often frustrated by the unresponsiveness of the system. All of us are exasperated by our Church's failures and inconsistencies, yet the idea of going elsewhere is out of the question. And woe betide the outsider who starts attacking it!

New Wine for Mature Wineskins

Undoubtedly, we Episcopalians sell ourselves short. Like children with their noses pressed against the toy store window, Christians in other traditions long for some of the blessings God has bestowed on us, whether it be the liturgy, the historic ordering of the Church, or the permission to be intellectually inquisitive. You only have to pick up a book like Frederick Buechner's *Telling Secrets* to discover the affection of this Presbyterian writer and minister for our liturgy.

Buechner is not the only Christian who looks longingly in our direction; for better or worse, others are compelled by the Holy Spirit to join us. For example, a leading executive of another denomination has told us that he expects to die in the Episcopal Church rather than the tradition in which he was raised and has worked for many years.

Of these and other such aspirations by a growing cross-section of American Christians, the Episcopal Church is a major beneficiary. There is a richness, depth, and potential balance in the Anglican expression of the Christian faith and life that seems inevitably to draw men and women out of other traditions. We have every expectation that this trend will continue to thrive during the remainder of this century.

On Easter Day 1990, 222 members of the Church of the King in Valdosta, Georgia, were confirmed. Formerly a Pentecostal congregation, Christ the King is now a mission of the Episcopal Diocese of Georgia. Although it was not the first Pentecostal congregation to be received into the Episcopal Church, the event received unprecedented media attention. Since that time Stanley White, their pastor, has received enquiries from all over the country from colleagues in independent or Pentecostal congregations, wondering how the Church of the King did it. White believes that the Episcopal Church is the wineskin waiting to be enriched and filled with the new wine being fermented in these other

Christian traditions. He envisions "the mushrooming ranks of independent congregations as a rich potential harvest," and speaks of "several pastors and several congregations who would like to come into the Episcopal Church if it could be worked out."[1]

From Rome to Canterbury

Meanwhile, from the opposite end of the ecclesiastical spectrum, there are well over 600 former Roman Catholic priests ministering in our midst: two are now diocesan bishops. While a variety of concerns, including the desire to marry, has brought them into our midst, most felt compelled to move when they could no longer live with Roman Catholic dogma and an inflexible ecclesiology.

Add to this number those who joined the Episcopal Church as lay persons and have subsequently been ordained, and the ranks of the clergy who were formerly Catholic increase considerably. We met a priest in Florida who is convinced that most Catholic seminaries tend to teach an Anglican rather than a Roman ecclesiology. He thinks we would be overwhelmed if too many pursued their theological propensities and migrated into our midst.

Throughout the United States, there are Episcopal parishes with large numbers of former Roman Catholics on the rolls. Several bishops, particularly those in the "Rust Belt," have identified congregations in their dioceses where it is hard to find anyone who did not begin life in the Roman communion. There is a deepening malaise in the Roman Catholic Church that could severely tax our ability to absorb their disenchanted in coming years. Often it is the brightest and best they are losing, such as one man we know who is a rising star in the diplomatic service. After years "away from God," he and his wife began a renewed spiritual search when their children were born. Each was so disenchanted by their Catholic upbringing that it was to the Episcopal Church they turned, where the seeds planted in childhood germinated and began to grow.

From Every Corner of Protestantism

Gather together any group of Episcopalians, but especially the clergy, and ask where they began their spiritual pilgrimage. As many as two-thirds will have begun life in Methodist, Baptist, Lutheran, or Presbyterian denominations, becoming Anglicans only in adulthood. Some were ordained in their former churches and chose to transfer, while others have come from conservative traditions like the Church of God, attracted by the richness of Anglicanism.

Deep within many American Christian hearts is a yearning for what most of us take for granted. Be it the respect given to the intellect, the roominess of our spirituality, or the integrity of the liturgy, the Episcopal Church continues to be a magnet for Christians wanting something more than the traditions of their upbringing could offer. Some have been educated beyond their past, others have been encouraged to make the break with it by the discontinuity of American society. Unlike almost anywhere else in the world, it is perfectly normal for Americans to find depth and substance by moving away from one's point of origin. As Robert Bellah writes, "Leaving tradition behind runs all the way through our [American] tradition."[2]

A few years ago, Robert Webber's book, *Evangelicals on the Canterbury Trail,* drew attention to the interest being shown in the Episcopal Church by well-educated conservative evangelicals. Today that trail is crowded with a cross-section of pilgrims, young and old, families and singles, looking for roots and a spiritual home. Small splinter groups have split from our tradition as a result of the contentious issues that have buffeted the Church, and some have journeyed from our midst into Roman Catholicism, but far greater numbers of clergy and laity are attracted by Episcopalianism. Although our statistics do not reflect this transfer growth because we have done a terrible job holding onto our own, losing hundreds of thousands, especially young people, to the spiritual wasteland of secularism, and less frequently to conservative evangelical churches, we believe there is great hope for the future growth of our Church.

It is hard to identify what it is within the genius of Anglicanism that attracts these spiritual travelers. Only a handful are merely passing through on their way to something else. Often these transients are seeking that chimera, the perfect church. Most who stumble across us in their search fall in love with Anglicanism and develop a passion for the Episcopal Church that matures into the fierce, indomitable loyalty of which our Canadian friend spoke. To these people, the idea of going back to where they came from is unacceptable. Anglicanism is compelling once it has been experienced.

The Magnetism of the Episcopal Church

We ask again, what is it that is bringing such people in?

One person might say "the liturgy," while another speaks of Episcopal Christians who helped in a crisis. The writings of C. S. Lewis have been an important introduction to Anglican Christianity for some, while others feel they have come home when they find an incarnation of the faith that allows them to take their minds seriously.

Whatever finally draws these searchers through our portals, beneath everything seems to be a search for identity, and never before has a nation sought identity as the United States does today. Part of the ferocious loyalty of Episcopalians might be because we have clearer idea than most in this topsy-turvy world, of who we are and where we have come from. In a dislocated society, people want to belong. "Because the United States is an achievement culture, identity is hard to come by," writes Tex Sample. "We do not have the deep traditional ties of a society where one's identity is determined by one's family or clan."[3]

Massive research into the changing face of American religion has led Princeton sociologist Robert Wuthnow to conclude that the rapid growth of higher education played a substantial role in reshaping people's religious preferences and commitments. "Unless one was an Episcopalian," he writes, "having been to college was extremely rare among the members of all denominations in the 1950's."[4] Since the 1960s, the education gap has been closing, which has created a pool of Christians uncomfortable with their family background. Even if they drop out of church for a while, as they marry and produce families, many seek new religious opportunities. As observed already, often it is those with good educational backgrounds who are finding their way into the Episcopal Church. During the 1990s, it is important that we make it attractive for others to follow them.

Wuthnow's research also suggests, however, that the better a person's education, the more likely he or she is to revert to a secular lifestyle. While we are in a strong position to garner new members by transfer from other traditions, we are more prone as well to lose the rising generation, as we lost many of the baby boomers to secular beliefs and lifestyle. Almost every parish priest we know has circumstantial evidence to back up Wuthnow's research.

Capitalizing on this Magnetism: The Agenda for the 90s

Holding onto our own, recovering those we have temporarily lost, while providing a spiritual haven for the growing numbers of well-informed people with a longing for God, is one of the major tasks before the Episcopal Church in the 1990s and beyond. If we are still as attractive as the evidence suggests, it is important that we capitalize upon our assets. While we expect this window of opportunity to remain open for a number of years, there is no guarantee this situation will last indefinitely. The generation presently in college, the children of the baby boomers, shows little propensity to ask the ultimate questions that lead people back into the Christian community.

This opportunity requires us to ask and answer some fundamental questions about ourselves. Are we a welcoming Church? Do we cater to the needs of young families, as well as singles of all ages? What of our approach to youth ministry and Christian education? We need to learn that our way of doing things is not the only way, and that we can benefit from the successes of other denominational and non-denominational groups, both evangelical and Roman Catholic.

This is an arena where the insights of newcomers from other traditions might be of help to us. Many have been raised in backgrounds where congregations have been successful in the areas outlined above. While they might have found much within their past that has been unsatisfactory, nevertheless they have continued to explore Christianity as a viable spiritual option. It is not impossible for newer Episcopalians to help us marry the best from, say, their Community Church upbringing, with the magnificence of our Anglican heritage.

As exciting as it is to know the Episcopal Church is so attractive to outsiders, their bonding within the life of the Church will require considerable open-handedness on our part if they are to be invited to play a full and vital role further enriching our common life. Are Episcopalians ready to be as hospitable and open-hearted? Remember, Stanley White of Valdosta thinks arriving Pentecostals provide new wine to put into our wineskins—inevitably the stresses they might put upon us could create situations where those skins are likely to split and burst. So here is the "$64,000 question": should the longings of Pentecostal Christians, Methodists, Southern Baptists, or Roman Catholics lead large numbers to shed their former allegiance and come into our midst, are we prepared to cope with them? When they have been formed, in preparation for confirmation and reception, and are fully part of our fellowship, are we willing to let them have their heads as they seek to modify our approach to mission and ministry? If we are not prepared to let the Episcopal Church grow in this way, we are turning our backs on the potential of our wonderful heritage.

Only a handful of these modern day pilgrims on the Canterbury trail join us out of disaffection from their past tradition. Most arrive at the end of a sincere search for a richer manifestation of the Christian faith. Having attracted this wide spectrum of pilgrims, Anglicanism has a breadth that enables it to absorb these individuals and set them free to exercise a wide variety of gifts and skills.

The arrival of large numbers of active believers from other traditions, filling our pews and contributing generously to our parish budgets, could lead to a blunting of our evangelistic determination. There is great danger in seeing our sole mission in terms of corralling people in from other churches, rather than reaching out to the unchurched and underprivileged.

While Episcopalianism appears an extremely attractive option to some of those from more conservative theological backgrounds, one of our correspondents, John H. Rogers of the Stanway Institute for Evangelism and World Mission, has presented another caveat that we should heed. In a personal letter he told us they will only continue to come "if we do not move in a dramatically liberal direction. As I read their mood, they wish to add the liturgical, sacramental, and historical dimensions without violating their evangelical convictions. A church that had lurched into an obviously liberal posture would not, I think, attract them."

What happens in this area of our life has several variables: the future courses taken by other churches, traditions, and denominations; and the future decisions of the Episcopal Church regarding fundamental theological and ethical stances. However, while denominationalism is of decreasing importance to American Christians, we expect that the Episcopal Church (through its social ministries, intellectual life, and spirituality) will continue to attract people who will find their faith enriched in our Communion. We expect to continue to welcome them and have them flourish in our midst for many years to come.

TRENDS TO WATCH

✚ We expect the Episcopal Church to retain its magnet-
ism for outsiders in the foreseeable future. People
from evangelical Protestant and from Roman Catholic
churches will continue to join the Episcopal Church.

✚ Believers from other traditions will be attracted to our
intellectual tradition, our rich liturgy, and the breadth
of our spirituality.

✚ The clarity of Anglican identity will be an important
factor in bringing in outsiders to our tradition.

✚ Flexibility and openness will be crucial in our incorpo-
ration of these new members.

CHAPTER TEN

A New Confidence in Evangelism

*A*s the second millennium of the Christian era draws to a close and the third bears down upon us, churches and para-church bodies all over our planet are redoubling their evangelistic efforts. At the very least they wish to give every human being an opportunity to hear the Good News before the year 2000 begins.

When the Society for Promoting Christian Knowledge (SPCK), the oldest Anglican mission agency, was founded in 1698, 454 million people were beyond the reach of Christian proclamation. At that time only 22.3% of the world's population were Christians, and all but a handful of these were Europeans or of European descent. Today 35% of the world's people call themselves Christian, yet the number that has yet to hear the Gospel has burgeoned to 1.4 billion.[1] When you add to this number those millions of people whose Christian profession is at best nominal, you can see the extent of our "mission field."

At home and abroad the task is enormous, but the Anglican Communion seems eagerly to have recommitted itself to the work of evangelism. The 1988 Lambeth Conference, with the following resolutions, called us to move forward in mission, evangelism, and church planting:

This Conference: calls for a shift to a dynamic missionary emphasis going beyond care and nurture to proclamation and services....

This Conference: recognizing that evangelism is the primary task given to the Church, asks each province and diocese of the Anglican Communion, in cooperation with other Christians, to make the closing years of this millennium a "Decade of Evangelism" with a renewed and united emphasis on making Christ known to the people of this world.[2]

There are parts of the worldwide Anglican family that do not need to be prodded into action. For example, in the last fifteen years the Diocese of Northern Borneo has been eagerly evangelizing inland Sabah and has seen 15,000 indigenous people come to faith in Christ.[3] However, in many other places the call of the Lambeth Conference demands a massive shift of emphasis. We are being called upon to move away from our primary focus of "care and nurture" to dynamic models for mission and outreach. Our leaders are asking all Anglican Christians, lay and ordained, to be agents of mission, and to use the coming years as a special opportunity for witness and evangelism.

What has been happening in parts of Africa, Latin America, and Asia, where Anglican believers are eager to "gossip the Gospel," must now find its way through the spiritual torpor in other parts of the Communion. New patterns of Christian discipleship are called for which, even if only partially successful, would dynamically transform the People of God in places like the United States.

There are whole armies of lay people in our Church waiting to be revitalized: to be energized with the fire of personal faith and a passion to serve Christ and make him known. We are being called to make a new beginning. Obviously, we have our work cut out for us.

Evangelism Phobia

By and large, American mainline churches enter the 1990s crippled by a phobia about the concept of evangelism. While some of these fears stem from a desire to dissociate themselves from the aggressive, tactless, and unreflective approach of many in the more fundamentalist Christian traditions, others stem from a misunderstanding or dislike of the whole idea of drawing people into a warm and loving relationship with Jesus Christ. Such churches have tended to see evangelism as the bailiwick of conservatives, evangelicals, and charismatics—not ourselves. It is no accident that Episcopalians sometimes talk of "the dreaded E-word" when referring to evangelism, and apologize profusely about the whole idea.

The Blue Book of reports and resolutions for the Phoenix General Convention reminded us of the priority of evangelism in the Standing Commission on Evangelism report:

> While the Prayer Book makes it clear that "Christians are to bear witness to Christ wherever they may be" (Book of Common Prayer p. 855), we have tended to see our relationship with God as a private matter, not to be shared or discussed with others. Evangelism (in any form) is frequently received by Episcopalians as an imposition. "What right do we have," many ask, "to force our religion on someone else?"...The sad fact is that in the Episcopal Church many have been sacramentalized without ever being evangelized. We need to call for decision not only from those beyond the Church but even from those within it."[4]

Attempts to change this paralyzing assumption have met with considerable passive resistance, and evangelism is only slowly being accepted. The majority of Episcopal Christians remain apprehensive and, by and large, lukewarm, although a faithful minority have embraced this call with enthusiasm, especially those who have been involved in the renewal movements.

In far too few parishes and dioceses have we seen much attempt to address this need in an intentional fashion. Not only are the laity of the Episcopal Church apprehensive, but we also find the clergy to be suspicious, often unwilling or unprepared to change the way they do things, often resistant to looking at new methodologies—even those suggested by members of their own parishes. It is no surprise, therefore, to find the laity often terrified of being involved in evangelistic activity and shy to nudge themselves toward participation.

What Lies Ahead?

We would be surprised to see a huge surge in evangelistic activity in the Episcopal Church in the near future. However, due to the impetus provided by the international Decade of Evangelism, and the habit that is already developing of trying to see our activities with "evangelistic eyes," we expect the profile of evangelism to rise during the 1990s.

During the remainder of this century we expect to see our people moving from apprehension about the whole concept toward a cautious acceptance of that fact the they are called to share with others God's redemption. As a result, preparations will take place that are likely to rehabilitate evangelism in the minds of the dubious. As this trend gathers pace, the membership slippage we continue to experience is likely to plateau and eventually new growth will come forth.

During the 1990s we expect increasing numbers of new parishes and missions to come into existence. The growth of these congregations will be the source of much encouragement. Furthermore, we expect various facets of the renewal movements to impact upon existing parishes that might be hemorrhaging membership, and a turn around will begin.

We anticipate that the groundwork being laid in the last decade of the twentieth century will start bearing significant evangelistic fruit in the twenty-first. Just as it has taken the stewardship movement time to begin changing the giving habits of Episcopalians, the higher profile being given through the Decade of Evangelism will definitely alter attitudes toward it. We expect to see increased creativity being used as individuals, parishes, and dioceses attempt to breathe new life into "gossiping the Gospel."

The Influence of the Renewal Movements

When dioceses have set up evangelism commissions, they have endeavored to involve renewal folk in them. Often these are the only committees to which renewal people are appointed by bishops and diocesan councils. At the same time, in many cases this has been their only interest at a diocesan level, or the only place where their particular contributions can appropriately be made.

Once established, such diocesan committees have often labored in the dark in vain, lacking enthusiastic support and becoming increasingly frustrated. These groups have focused far too much on "how to do evangelism," giving little thought to theology, and sometimes being too apologetic to talk vigorously about conversion and transformation. Moreover, very often they have gleaned resources and ideas about evangelism that do not translate well into the culture of the Episcopal Church. It has only been recently that the national Office on Evangelism has begun to produce helpful resources for the Decade of Evangelism. The acceptance of these assets is often hampered by the suspicion of renewal people toward anything produced by the Episcopal Church Center.

The result has often been that instead of encouraging evangelism, enthusiasts have instead turned off their potential constituency. Starved of funds and resources, these committees lack recognition in the diocese and are sometimes treated with outright hostility. The result is a depressed group of people striving to get the Episcopal Church to take evangelism seriously. Like a string quartet playing Bach at a cocktail party, they are seldom heard.

We believe that despite their shortcomings, renewal movements in our church have already paved the way for this Decade. They have and will continue to accelerate the change coming over this church. Cursillo, catechumenate processes, Faith Alive!, Happening, Evangelism Explosion, and Episcopal Renewal Ministries—just to name a few of the movements—have all played important roles for two decades. Added to them must be the profound impact being made by the evangelistic ministries of individuals like John Guest of the Diocese of Pittsburgh, and Bryan Green, the octogenarian evangelist from England. It is impossible not to see God's hand at work in these ministries.

Such a selection of ways to proclaim the Gospel appears to be the way that God is calling us to present Jesus in the power of the Holy Spirit. Such is the vision for a Decade of Evangelism presented in the Blue Book at Phoenix in July 1991, as it lifts up the examples of "transformed individuals," "radiant congregations," and "visionary dioceses" as illustrations of the renewal at work to move God's people to evangelism. This exciting report, the best prepared and the most encouraging to come out of the Phoenix Convention, cleared the way for the passage of a series of achievable resolutions that we as a church are now called to implement.

Much of what was observed from Lambeth and its inspiring leadership in the arena of evangelism points up a radical changing of the agenda for the Episcopal Church. If we are to be in step with the rest of the Anglican Communion, we are being challenged to rethink a whole variety of aspects of our life as a church.

Shaking the Structures

The structure of our church appears more and more to hamper our vision, and the institutional nature of our body seems to throw countless obstacles in the way as we attempt to move to a mission model for action at parish, diocesan, provincial, and national church levels.

We are certain that as we attempt to rethink our part in the re-evangelization of the church and the evangelization of the world, both structure and agenda will be profoundly affected. Looking beneath the frustrations and disappointments of the Phoenix Convention, we were able to see the beginnings of change. From the House of Bishops and throughout the whole Church, the questioning of present structures and the way decisions are made is not going to disappear.

At Phoenix we began to see how important the grass-roots organizations really are. As they redouble their efforts in ministry, their work and very existence will continue to raise questions of systemic importance. It is hard to overestimate their impact on the future of the Episcopal Church.

A Spectrum of Models

The Decade of Evangelism has been approached in a variety of ways around the Church. There are those who are celebrating it with "grandstand events," while at the other extreme there are Episcopalians who throw up their hands in horror, saying "We cannot think of a thing to do!" Perhaps one of the earliest discoveries during this decade of exploration has been that it is not a "thing" that we try to do, but an ongoing, life-changing process.

At present there seem to be no attempts on the horizon for a denomination-wide evangelistic program—partly because of the individualism and congregationalism of Episcopalians, and partly, perhaps, because of the low level of trust in denomination-led agendas. This fact was verified in the study of the Presbyterian Church (USA) undertaken by the Lilly Endowment, indicating this to be true in all the American mainline churches.

There are a multitude of approaches to evangelism that are open to the Holy Spirit. Some have very long-term goals and objectives, while others seek to enthuse and move us quickly to a committed response, one that will shape the Decade so that its effects reach far into the next century. Planting, watering, re-enlivening, and encouraging for the proclamation of the Good News in both words and deeds may be the most fruitful way forward.

Certainly where catechumenal processes are being taken seriously, the development of evangelistic outreach by the baptized is seen to be dependent upon bringing persons to conversion or recommitment. Their faith invigorated, it is then the task of the parish to form them in Christ, equipping them for ministry in their particular sphere, using the God-given gifts with which they have been endowed.

Focusing on our Distinctiveness

An emerging and parallel trend that we are tracking among Episcopalians is their desire to ascertain what is a distinctly Anglican or Episcopal way to handle the evangelistic process. At its worst this is a not-so-subtle sectarianism, yet at its best it is an attempt to develop an apologetic. Why are we professing and preaching our faith as Episcopalians and not as members of some other Christian tradition? It is a process of raising up, highlighting if you will, the distinguishing marks of our Christian style, without feeling we have a need to apologize.

It is our belief that this search for Episcopal distinctiveness has evolved from our deep involvement in ecumenical discussion and activity, where there has sometimes been an attempt to find the lowest common denominator for the union of churches. This has led to a "watering down" of the particularities, leading many to sense that we are being less than frank about those elements of the faith that are important to us. Perhaps this is the reason for radical changes that have been made in the Consultation on Church Union (COCU) document as it has attempted to discover what is "acceptable" to the member churches.

Ecumenism is on Hold

In our original preparation for this book we had anticipated that the ecumenical efforts were going to continue as a major trend during this decade, perhaps even raising its profile. There were signs as the 1980s drew to a close that rapid progress would be made toward new forms of unity during the 1990s. We no longer see this happening with much velocity. The expectations of the 1980s are not being fulfilled, leading us to believe that ecumenism will be on a "low burner" for most of the remainder of the century.

The prime example of this must be the proposed Concordat between the Episcopal Church and the Evangelical Lutheran Church in America (ELCA). The relationship between Episcopalians and Lutherans, which had moved forward rapidly and seemed to be teetering on the brink of a historic agreement, cooled during 1991. The ELCA, still adjusting to its own tri-church union, decided it was not ready to act on the Concordat, and asked for a two-year breathing space, although they have agreed to study it.

Immediately the impetus slowed, momentum toward union has been lost, and enthusiasm for such a close relationship seems to be waning in both churches. While we believe there will be continued good relationships between Episcopal and Lutheran Christians, we do not anticipate this potential liaison will have a major impact on our lives during the remainder of this century. Such unions, as we can see from the ELCA internal merger, use up huge amounts of energy as the new structures settle in, adjust, and come to terms with themselves. Such efforts are bound to detract from evangelistic focus and outreach.

Our dialogue with the Roman Catholic Church, both in this country and internationally, appears to have gone about as far as it can, as we see from the Vatican's belated response to the joint reports of the Anglican-Roman Catholic International Consultation (ARCIC). The lack of enthusiastic conversations and cooperation at the local level reflects more conservative episcopal appointments being made in the United States by the Vatican, putting into leadership positions those for whom ecumenism is not a high priority.

We believe we are being generous when we observe that COCU "hangs on" with an equal lack of enthusiasm and continued confusion of objectives. We do not anticipate that any proposed union between the participating churches will come to anything, and it certainly would not accelerate evangelistic fervor! Often proposed unions between Protestant and Anglican churches look too much like survival tactics as two declining entities attempt to form a larger but dying body. Many of those Episcopalians most eager to respond to the challenge of the Decade of Evangelism have deep misgivings about aspects of ecumenism and are quite happy to see it sidelined.

While we do not rule out surprises, concordats, partner-ships, and unions are a lower priority on the Episcopal Church's agenda, and certainly would do little to bring new-ness of life to our churches, to their mission, and to their ability to proclaim the Gospel. Too often in the past we have allowed ourselves to be distracted by the institutional aspects of ecumenism, and these have diverted us from the task of mission. Perhaps it is a blessing that so many interchurch relationships are on hold, giving us time to concentrate on evangelism.

Grass Roots Ecumenism

While national and international ecumenical consult-ations will not cease entirely, the focus of partnership will be on the local level, where we can come to a better under-standing of our call to mission. Examples of local coopera-tion for evangelism can be seen when Episcopal parishes join with others to sponsor a Billy Graham campaign, or in-volve themselves in multichurch missions led by the Epis-copal priest-evangelist, John Guest. In many parts of the country such activities have not only facilitated the spread of the Gospel, but have engendered strong and lasting inter-church relationships.

This trend toward building cooperative relationships at the local level contrasts markedly with efforts to bring about mergers at a national level. It is part of that much larger movement away from hierarchical structures toward net-works will be outlined in a later chapter. Ecumenism at the local level endorses the interrelatedness of the lives of those who may belong to different churches, but who see their call first and foremost to be evangelists.

What about the Decade of Evangelism, Then?

Although we have identified some fears about evangelism, there are signs of potential growth in the Church as we look at the overall picture. There are many parishes that are thriving, and are experiencing a deepening of faith and community life together with a growth in numbers. In these parishes, evangelism often has a high priority and there is an expectation that people will respond when the Gospel is meaningfully proclaimed, and when they are being nourished by prayer, the sharing of the sacrament, and the opening of the Scriptures.

Numerical growth most often comes through the development of new congregations. Unless there is an unusual Christian spiritual awakening or a radical change in demographics, growth is less often seen in parishes more than twenty years old. The General Convention placed before us a vision in which parishes and dioceses will attempt to establish one thousand new congregations before the end of the year 2000. This in turn has stimulated many dioceses to begin a church-planting ministry. We encourage Episcopalians to focus their resources on the development of hundreds of new missions during the remaining years of the Decade of Evangelism.

With no national goals, we all been left to our own devices. Although in the past that has often translated into doing little or nothing at all, we believe it is now possible that the grassroots will begin to assert themselves in the wake of this broader loss of nerve among the Church's leadership.

While the trend in the Decade of Evangelism is toward preparation for the future, those dioceses that have done some serious groundwork for evangelism and formation will see results in this decade or the first years of the next century. Such dioceses may inspire others to see that time spent in preparing their people for mission through conversion, renewal, and re-formation is well worth the effort.

There is much we can learn from our sisters and brothers in other churches. Already many Episcopal parishes have benefited from the Evangelism Explosion program pioneered by Coral Ridge Presbyterian Church, Fort Lauderdale, Florida. Even such stereotypically reclusive Christians as the Wisconsin Evangelical Lutheran Synod have things to teach us. Their "Come to the W.E.L.S." evangelistic campaign that invites people to the Wisconsin Evangelical Lutheran Seminars may have something to teach us in our search. We have no need to copy exactly what others do, but neither is there any need to reinvent the wheel just because they are different from us.

All this talk ultimately comes down to our willingness to be open to the presence and working of the Holy Spirit in our lives. It is God who converts people, calls them into his community, empowers, challenges, touches, and changes. It is up to us whether we respond—giving ourselves lock, stock, and barrel! God will work through us in evangelism as we make ourselves ever more available to him.

Yet embracing such openness in the life of the Episcopal Church will have to mean systemic change. What happens in the next ten years will demonstrate whether we have really given evangelism a higher priority. It will involve a major shift of perceptions and of direction. Those studying for ordained ministry must be convinced that evangelism is of the essence of the Gospel, and they need to be formed and equipped to enable the baptized for their ministry in God's mission.

Evangelism must become a focus of parish-based ministry. It must be lifted up at the local congregational level in every aspect of our life: from forming our young children to inspiring adults to fulfill their call to be followers and witnesses to Jesus Christ.

Evangelistic Vision and the National Church

Evangelism has a far higher priority at the Episcopal Church Center than it did ten years ago. It appears we are finally taking seriously congregational development, the establishment of new parishes, and Christian formation. Meanwhile, the Evangelism Unit is increasingly effective in communicating teaching and methodology at parish and diocesan levels.

The time is ripe for us to be open to new vision and new approaches to evangelism. We pray these new developments will have a profound impact at the grass roots. If they are to be properly supported at a national church level, it will take a commensurate amount of funding for staff, essential research, and the development of parish-based programs.

To date, our words and actions do not gibe. The triennial budget coming out of the Phoenix Convention set aside some $600,000 for development in the (albeit needed) area of economic justice, while funding for the Standing Commission on Evangelism was set at only $45,000 for the same three-year period. It is our hope that some balance in these two priority items can be injected by the next General Convention in Indianapolis in 1994.

T R E N D S   T O   W A T C H

✚ Episcopalians' fear of evangelism will slowly moderate in the 1990s.

✚ We expect to see parishes increasingly take the shift toward a mission model of operation seriously.

✚ There will be a lessening in the rate of membership decline, but there is little sign of significant new growth until early in the next century.

✚ Even without specific national goals, there will be an acceleration of new church planting.

✚ As the groundwork for the future is laid, we expect to see the renewal movements playing a major role in this aspect of church life.

✚ Institutional ecumenism will experience a lull, but grass-roots ecumenism, especially where it involves evangelism and outreach, will flourish.

CHAPTER ELEVEN

The Continued Priority of Stewardship

*U*ntil the middle 1970s Episcopalians were, with rare exceptions, mediocre givers to the ministry of the Church. Since that time a great deal has changed for the better. While it still has a long way to go, since that time the Episcopal Church has improved its stewardship performance considerably, and we expect this emphasis on stewardship to continue for the foreseeable future.

In 1988, the last year for which there were complete figures, the Episcopal Church was the best-giving denomination for churches with a million members or more, only bettered on the giving scale by some of the small, tightly-knit conservative denominations. There are many who delight in identifying the things that are obviously wrong in the Church's life, but here is something that points up a healthy facet of our common identity.

Much of this change is due to the efforts of Thomas H. Carson, Jr., stewardship officer of the national church from 1978 to 1989. The *Venture in Mission* program, a capital campaign initiated by the former Presiding Bishop, John M. Allin, also played a significant role in our progress toward better stewardship.

Until Dr. Carson came on board at the Church Center, talk and action about stewardship were patchy in the life of the Church. Perhaps the preeminent example of stewardship leadership in the 1970s was to be found in the Diocese of Alabama, which hatched what became known as "The Alabama Plan."[1] Each congregation was challenged to move toward spending 50% of its income beyond itself, a goal many achieved. Obviously, it required a significant boost in individual pledges.

In 1982, the General Convention, meeting in New Orleans, endorsed "the biblical tithe as the standard of giving," and in the years following many diocesan conventions passed resolutions that echoed, sometimes even strengthened, the leadership given by General Convention. Extraordinary as it may seem, never before had the Episcopal Church talked about tithing and affirmed that 10% of one's income returned to the Lord is the biblical standard for giving.

Armed with biblical teaching and this resolution, Tom Carson and his staff were able to provide structure to the joy of giving in the life of the Church. They crisscrossed the country, traveling hundreds of thousands of miles each year, establishing a strong stewardship network, training leadership and providing a new enthusiasm for the ministry of giving. Carson built a staff team and a team of volunteers to whom the Church owes a tremendous debt. In 1974 parish giving was $315 million; ten years later it had risen over 250%, and as we entered the final decade of the century this total was up to $1.2 billion. This is despite the fact that an average of only 58% of Episcopalians pledge, a fact that indicates enormous potential for future growth.

Today few Episcopalians would openly question the tithe as the standard for Christian giving, although relatively few have yet personally responded to this challenge. The dramatic rise in stewardship has in fact started leveling off, but this biblical standard is unlikely to be seriously challenged during the coming decade. Not only are more clergy preaching the joys of realistic stewardship, but many dioceses have also added staff persons whose full-time work is in this area, be it to encourage regular giving or to enable planned gifts and long-term development strategies. However, looking at the average pledge of most Episcopalians, we have to ask in all honesty whether we have gotten beyond mere lip-service to the concept of the biblical tithe.

We recently discovered an interesting example of the discontinuity between stewardship belief and practice. The leadership of a particular diocese, when surveyed in preparation for stewardship training, indicated an 11.5% level of giving to charitable causes, yet only 4% was specifically earmarked for the ministry of the Church. We surmise this might be a higher level of giving than the rank-and-file in most parishes.

During the coming decade, we expect to see a renewed emphasis on stewardship, with an increased concentration on planned giving. Episcopal Christians are being encouraged to look beyond the implications of tithing for their immediate income, to the manner in which they handle their material wealth when they pass from this world to the next. In addition, it is being recognized that a generation of people of significant means and generosity has started to come to an end, and so the Church is seeking ways to enable them to share some of their blessings with the wider Christian family. Unfortunately, many charitable organizations and educational bodies are at least a decade ahead of the Episcopal Church in soliciting our membership for their often worthy causes.

Even if leadership from the Episcopal Church Center weakens due to financial stringencies, we do not expect efforts toward better stewardship to fade away as we enter the new century, but to broaden and become more comprehensive in their understanding of this task.

Whither Stewardship?

During the seventies and early eighties, when the Church talked about stewardship it was generally referring to financial giving, despite the fact that we spent a great deal of time emphasizing that stewardship had to do with "time, treasure, and talents." This emphasis upon money was probably necessary because for too long we had not given adequate attention to the "treasure" component of that trio.

However, during recent years we have started to see a deliberate widening of our understanding of stewardship. Today we are looking way beyond "time, treasure, and talents." Increased environmental awareness, the inequitable distribution of wealth throughout the world, and other such global issues have become part of the equation. Given the world's finite resources we have started asking questions about the correct interpretation of God's injunction in Genesis, chapter 1, to "have dominion" over the earth. Sensitive Episcopalians, like Christians from other traditions, have realized that dominion has given way to exploitation. We have treated the world as a source of resources to be quarried rather than a trust to be looked after — if humanity is to have a future, this approach must change.

We expect a major struggle in coming years as we attempt to integrate faith with economics and search for a sustainable lifestyle for a finite planet. As the depth of the environmental crisis is realized, questions about the advisability of free market economics, and the part it has played in brutalizing the planet, are sure to arise. During the coming two decades we expect to see the Christian churches in the West going through periods of deep heart-searching as they wrestle their way toward what John V. Taylor called "the theology of enough."

In his prophetic book written nearly twenty years ago, *Enough is Enough*, Bishop Taylor, recently retired as Bishop of Winchester, England, called into question "our society's reluctance to impose the most obvious restrictions" upon itself in order to curtail the rape of the earth.[2] He continues,

> My object is not to calculate where we shall be by the end of the century, but to disclose what manner of civilization we have become and what kind of spirit it is that possesses and drives us....My concern is diagnosis more than prognosis, and I believe that what is wrong is not so much what we are doing as the frame of reference within which we are doing it, or, if you like, not so much our way of grabbing at things as our way of looking at things. Our sickness is more like eye disease than heart disease. But don't for a minute imagine that that is less serious, for didn't Jesus say: "If the eyes are bad, your whole body will be in darkness. If then the only light you have is darkness, the darkness is doubly dark?"[3]

In the Episcopal Church we began the "stewardship journey" in the seventies by looking at the implications of our faith in Jesus Christ upon our pocketbooks. This was an excellent place in which to start, but in coming years we will be asked to move far beyond this. The debate will be frenetic because the survival of our planet, the human race, and all the species of animals and plants entrusted to us by God will be at stake. It is the kind of debate that will move far beyond our limited present theological, social, and political labeling. We hazard a guess that the present categorizing of "liberal," "conservative," and "moderate" will mean less and less as the debate progresses.

With the rest of humankind, we will be working our way toward a holistic understanding of our relationship to the world around us, and what it means to bring about the *shalom* of the Bible. Shalom is true peace and harmony among our race, all creatures, and "this fragile earth, our island home," and is in significant contrast to present dissonance. It is a tricky path we will be treading, but one whose dimension is of vital importance to the future of the world, and the role the Christian Faith plays within it.

Awareness of a gathering storm is surfacing in the councils of the Church. Beginning at the General Convention in Detroit, Michigan, in 1988, and continuing through the Phoenix Convention, it became apparent that peace, justice, environment, and stewardship issues were merging as various commissions addressed the rising environmental crisis. Many are saying that the 1990s may be the Decade of the Environment rather than the Decade of Evangelism!

The following is to be found in the report presented to the 1991 General Convention by the Standing Commission on Stewardship and Development:

> Environmental stewardship, like all Christian stewardship, must become a way of life....Each Christian, in response to God's teaching, should embark on a course of environmental responsibility.[4]

The questioning by Christian theologians of our present attitudes toward wealth, lifestyle, and the environment became more insistent throughout the 1980s. Several leading thinkers are venturing to raise pertinent and fundamental challenges in their recent writings. M. Douglas Meeks, a Methodist who has worked as a consultant with the national church Stewardship Office, asks us to look at our role as stewards of God's household.

> Seeking to live the economy of God, the congregation can contribute to a more just public household....It is a resurrection household that God is struggling to build. The

decisive fact is that the resurrection changes the household rules.[5]

We can expect this deeper and further reaching "stewardship journey" to be far more traumatic than anything we have encountered before. We can safely say that reaching after the biblical tithe has been child's play when compared to the challenge ahead, as we broaden the base of our understanding of this facet of Christian lifestyle. We expect significant controversies, deep heart-searching, and such honest but profound differences of opinion that extraordinary pain will be experienced before they are resolved. There will be no easy way round the resulting altercations.

The Way Ahead

During the next ten to twenty-five years, we would not be surprised to see the emergence at a popular level of a Franciscan style of spirituality, as Episcopal Christians are forced to explore the implications of a simpler lifestyle. This is bound to clash with the affluent approach to life that reflects the ideology of success that has predominated in the United States during the last century or more.

The cry that will increasingly go up will be a call to radical discipleship, akin to nothing we have experienced in the West in many generations. Our materialism will be called into question as never before, not only by our Christian faith, but also by the growing numbers of increasingly poor and downtrodden people in the Two-Thirds World. The part the Church plays in responding to their challenge will determine what sort of order is likely to prevail in the USA and elsewhere on this small planet a century from now.

Meeting in a college auditorium in Brockport, New York, on a cold November day in 1988, the Convention of the Diocese of Rochester overwhelmingly passed a resolution affirming that "stewardship is the main work of the Church." The resolution went on to say that "stewardship is an adventure, an expedition into the kingdom where we find our lives through losing them for the sake of the Gospel....It offers us a way to begin breaking the bonds of consumption that involve us, often unwittingly, in perpetuating injustice and oppression." [6]

Those words, probably echoed in many other dioceses throughout the country, are prophetic. Tithing, in which Episcopalians have made a reasonably good start, is merely the first step on a journey that will take us into uncharted yet joyful territory for our lives and lifestyles in the years ahead.

TRENDS TO WATCH

✚ We expect to see a slow but steady growth in the practice of tithing.

✚ Developing creative methods of planned giving will be an important focus for stewardship in the years ahead.

✚ Environmental stewardship, and the relationship between stewardship , ecology, and justice, will become an increasingly important issue in our teaching and acting as communities and individuals.

✚ We anticipate a steady trend toward simplicity of lifestyle as Episcopalians begin to define the concept of stewardship far more broadly than they have in the past.

CHAPTER TWELVE

The Spread of Single-Issue Organizations

merican society is fragmenting. The disruptive effects of this massive divide are seen in almost every aspect of our nation's life, and reverberate as well through the daily life and governance of the Episcopal Church.

For many Episcopalians this has not been an easy time as we have sought to make sense of the issues of our age. We have watched enrolled membership dwindle by some 30% since 1965, and we seem powerless to halt the slide. These alarming figures require skilled analysis if they are to be properly understood. Certainly the statistics raise flags telling us something is drastically wrong and has yet to be put right, but there is more to them than at first meets the eye. A very useful exercise that ought to be undertaken is a detailed analysis of all this information so that we might grasp the realities with which we are confronted, rather than making wild extrapolations on the basis of numbers alone.

We fiercely contest the implications in the title of Wade Clark Roof's *Wall Street Journal* article, "The Episcopalian Goes the Way of the Dodo."[1] Nevertheless, particularly in the Northeast, we have seen a startling decline that ought to leave the Church asking some fundamental questions about the nature of its faith and ministry. One factor in our apparent numerical loss is stricter methods of recording and the fact that diocesan quotas and assessments are increasingly levied on a head count. Even taking this into account, however, and even if a valid "prophetic" ministry does not necessarily woo great crowds, we still cannot explain away the whole of our loss in those terms. The only conclusion to be reached is that in many places the Episcopal Church is not witnessing for Christ to a spiritually hungering world, a point that has not been missed by large segments of the Church.

Most parishes on the more conservative end of the Episcopal spectrum know the pain of those who have found the comprehensiveness of the Episcopal Church difficult to handle. There are few priests who have not watched in distress as they have seen members of their congregation say "goodbye" and move to a more theologically conservative denomination. Then there is the additional pain caused by those who have joined a smaller Anglican schismatic group or have entered the Roman Catholic Church because they are opposed to the ordination of women.

The tragedy of this exodus is that we have often lost men and women who could have played a crucial role in enriching us. Whether the last straw has been the imagined "unbelief" of their rector, an ill-considered pronouncement or action by a bishop, or an objection to the policies of the national church, they have shaken Episcopal dust from their feet and turned their backs on us.

It is incumbent upon those of us who are left to learn from these departures in order to prevent such slippage in the future. It is important for us to ask searching questions of those who are leaving and be willing to listen to honest answers. Not only will we hear some unpleasant opinions about ourselves, but we will also discover what part we might have played in bringing about their departures. While it is important that we learn from these losses to other denominations, they have still been a relatively small segment of the mix. We are more likely to lose people to a secular lifestyle lacking contact with organized religion altogether than to another religious group.

Infuriated Conservatives and Crusading Liberals

There are thousands who are anxious about the various twists and turns the Church is taking, but remain inside to combat the "evil" they perceive enveloping us. Such people make up the core of various conservative and traditionalist single-issue groups that have sprung up recently. Each is focused to challenge what is perceived to be inappropriate positions taken by those within the Church, especially the "establishment." Over the years these groups have become more vocal and more sophisticated in their marketing and lobbying as they have sought to change the direction the Church is taking. Their membership is a mixture of old-style traditionalists and conservatives deeply influenced by the renewal movements. We focus upon them because we believe they will have an increasingly high profile in the years ahead.

Ironically, the newer, conservative groups clash head on with single-issue groups from the liberal quadrant of Church life. Unlike their liberal counterparts, however, they have a large constituency and openly express the opinions of an extensive segment in the pews. An indication of this is their ability to raise substantial funding to promote their point of view. Liberal groups are more likely to represent a small but activist elite who are determined to see the Church respond to their agenda.

Sometimes it is fury and disgust with the single-issue groups of the left that have compelled those on the right to take the actions they do. In this way, the councils of the

Church reflect the push and pull of Capitol Hill more and more every day. Yet beneath the battle something far more significant is happening: a struggle for the soul of the Church between the liberal and conservative ends of the spectrum, which (as Robert Wuthnow writes) "has roots in a different views of the Bible, in different styles of moral reasoning, and even in different concepts of spirituality."[2]

While liberals consider themselves prophetic, walking in the footsteps of Christ as they attack injustice and systemic evil, conservatives believe many of the policies they espouse reflect a capitulation to the spirit of modernity as it dictates their agenda. They see it as a form of syncretism. On the other hand, when liberals look at conservatives, they label them uncaring and unreflective fundamentalists, upholders of the status quo, bigots, and hypocrites. On the surface of things, it appears we have a stand-off!

However, while liberal groups are extremely vocal and have had considerable influence during the last generation, proponents of liberal policies, issues, and lifestyles now appear to be losing ground. Although successive General Conventions continue to be managed by those on the left through of the present appointive structure, the rank and file of the Church are moving progressively toward the center. In addition, the agenda of more liberal Episcopalians seems to be increasingly out of step with the anxieties of the rest of the Church's membership.

Integrity, which voices the concerns of the gay and lesbian lobby, has been astute in its use of the media and political processes, but they speak for a relatively small group of activists within the Church. Even with this expertise, at this point in time they have been unable to convince the Church of the rightness of their cause. Conservatives think this organization wields power far beyond its numbers, because it has been listened to by those who shape opinion and structure the program and budget of the Church.

Whether this is true will be debated for several years to come. We believe in the future that the organizations that will press forward the fastest to reform the Church's agenda will be those on the conservative end of the spectrum, including the Prayer Book Society, the Episcopal Synod of America, and Episcopalians United. In a slightly different vein is the National Organization of Episcopalians for Life (NOEL), which speaks against abortion from a Christian context. Then there are a myriad of other smaller entities that focus on specific issues.

As hinted already, one of the reasons for the explosion of agencies on the right is the perception by many at the local level that the prevailing views of the official spokespersons of the Church are at odds with their own more traditional values. The tendency is to consider every statement emanating from the Episcopal Church Center with suspicion. Despite protestations of inclusiveness from the Church's leadership, there is often a significant gulf between the presuppositions of those who speak and those who hear them in the pews.

Rather than being pushed from the Episcopal nest by their more radical sisters and brothers, conservatives have now turned, are standing their ground, and are fighting back for their agenda. We are in the midst of a debate that will determine the future of Anglican faith and polity in North America. We expect the battle to ebb and flow for at least the next decade and beyond. However, there is every reason to believe the Church entering the new century will have moved further to the center and away from both extremes.

Anglicanism has always permitted latitude, fostering an environment where Christians have been allowed to differ from one another and still remain in fellowship. We believe such comprehensiveness is healthy, but the questions for today are: "What, if any, are the acceptable limits? How liberal or conservative can you be in your theology and ecclesiology, and still be considered loyal to the genius of our tradition?"

We believe that during the 1990s these questions will be debated, sometimes with great passion and anger, and they will focus on sexuality issues. The issues of appropriate sexual morality, of the place and role of practicing homosexuals, and of the rights of the unborn and of women, will act as lightning rods for this dialogue. We suspect it will be a very long time before these controversies die down.

Maybe as we wrestle with these issues at home, we will find ourselves listening more closely to voices from the Two-Thirds World, the cutting edge of the Anglican Communion, to understand our tradition properly. If this happens, we are certain that neither the right nor the left will necessarily like what they hear.

A New Style of Leadership

One of the most crucial issues facing the leadership of the Episcopal Church as we move to the end of the century is how these various interest groups can be handled and enabled to debate enormous issues. At present each side yells at the other without listening to what is said by the other. If a proper debate is not facilitated, this polarization could further rip the Church apart.

Those on the right have legitimate grievances, for the forming of single-issue organizations illustrates this fact. As the decade proceeds and conservative principles gain momentum, is it possible that the most frustrated single-issue lobbies may become those on the left instead?

In 1988, the Prayer Book Society, one of the older single-issue groups on the right, was prominent at the General Convention because of the huge red billboards that greeted bishops and deputies on the road into town from the Detroit International Airport, decrying the policies that had "shrunk" the Episcopal Church. The Prayer Book Society's presence in our midst is, perhaps, a reminder that we have been high-handed in the manner we have consigned the 1928 Book of Common Prayer to oblivion. This was the book that nurtured the faith of several generations of Episcopalians and is in direct descent from the Reformation Prayer Books of 1549 and 1552, and the first Prayer Book of the American Church framed in 1789. Rich in content and deeply loved, perhaps the Church should have been less rigid and more tolerant in the way it treated this venerable source of spirituality and worship.

Now that the 1979 Book of Common Prayer has been generally accepted, maybe one of the questions the presence of the Prayer Book Society raises for the 1990s is, "Is it time to give honor where honor is due to the 1928 Book?" We believe this could be done without detracting from the continuing Prayer Book revision, but at the same time offering a pastoral concession to many in the Church. While the numbers of those elderly who love the old Prayer Book are shrinking with each passing year, much pain could be alleviated if their alienation from the mainstream of the Church's life were somewhat relieved. We expect there to be a steady rumble of background static throughout the coming years for some sort of reconciliation with the 1928 standard of worship.

The Episcopal Synod of America is a reminder to us that there is a considerable minority within the Episcopal Church that is not happy with the decision to ordain women to the priesthood made in 1976. This group was further aroused by the consecration of Barbara Harris as Suffragan Bishop of Massachusetts in 1989, and is now unfortunately calling into question the orders of all those ordained by her. More recently they have included in their agenda defenses of trinitarian theology, traditional sexual morality, and the Bible itself.

For members of the Synod, a traditional all-male understanding of priesthood and biblical truth are part and parcel of one another. They are convinced that in ordaining women we have erred grievously, and that whatever the arguments made by everyone from the Archbishop of Canterbury down, tradition and antiquity are on their side. Women's ordination is to them another example of the Church's sell-out to modernity.

The Synod has a reputation for being prickly, and they are looking for ways to insulate themselves from the jeopardizing of apostolicity that Bishop Harris's presence represents. For several years they have lobbied for an additional, nongeographical province of the Church as a solution to the ecclesiological dilemma they perceive, and are now championing the concept of a missionary diocese. Their presence prompts us to remember that we have not always acted with generosity toward those who question the wisdom of women in ordained ministry. Unless the tolerance implicit in Anglican principles is applied during coming years, we are certain there could be a parting of the ways with some of their number. However, if we are to stay together, and we believe that is what Christian unity demands, then *both* sides of the argument must be prepared to yield something to the other.

Episcopalians United (EU) has garnered for itself the reputation of a rabble-rouser. Several direct mail pieces that it has sent out over the years have been unnecessarily blunt and have resorted to misrepresentation and scare tactics.

Still, their capacity to gather over 20,000 members and raise significant sums of money suggests they have touched raw nerves. Even if they do not say it tactfully, EU is telling us loud and clear that Episcopalians at the grass-roots level are dissatisfied with the performance and stance of the leadership of the Church.

In January 1986, representatives of evangelical, charismatic, and catholic renewal in the Episcopal Church gathered at the Three R's Conference in Winter Park, Florida. Episcopalians United is the step-child of this gathering, although it does not by any means represent the opinions of all present on that occasion. In recent years, it has played a strong role in attacking attempts by the Church to move away from traditional sexual morality, and it has resisted the pressure to use and accept inclusive language liturgies. While EU does not share the same public distrust of women priests as both the Prayer Book Society and Episcopal Synod of America, they are deeply resentful of feminism and of philosophies and movements that might be considered its fellow-travelers.

Their sometimes simplistic presentation of the issues seems designed, at times, to anger the Episcopal Church's "establishment," but it sounds a deep chord with many who feel frustrated and believe their voices are not listened to. As long as the press continues to focus on the more outrageous activities of a handful of members of the Episcopal Church, and as long as its leadership tacitly consents to these positions, we can expect such organizations to flourish, even if their actual effectiveness is limited.[3] When EU vocally opposes the extreme opinions of a "liberal cabal" that appears to them to be holding onto power at all costs, its stridency inflames the anxiety levels of loyal but disaffected Church members. But suggestions of a wholesale takeover by the homosexual lobby and personal attacks on the integrity of the Presiding Bishop only add to the polarization of the Church.

Is there a solution?

In coming years the Church, both at the leadership and grass-roots levels, needs to listen with care not just to the liberal groups, but also to those like the ones mentioned in this chapter. Inclusiveness is a fine idea only if everyone is included. While it is impossible to make everyone happy, destructive tensions would certainly be reduced if every voice felt it was being heard.

Presiding Bishop Browning has worked earnestly since the outset of his episcopate to validate his statement that "there are no outsiders" in the Episcopal Church, although his continued communication with conservative groups has not always been appreciated by either them or their liberal counterparts. We believe the ecclesiology, theology, and essential generosity of Anglican principles equip this tradition to cope with the gulf that has widened between liberals and conservatives. However, if we turn our back on the comprehensiveness of our tradition implicit in our past, then there is no telling what damage still may be done.

Single-issue groups are now part of the warp and woof of the Episcopal Church and are unlikely to go away. They are not only representative of the transition the Church is making from hierarchies to networks, but also express strongly held views.

T R E N D S   T O   W A T C H

✚ Liberal and conservative single-issue groups will remain polarized, and their clash is likely to become increasingly bitter in coming years. The sexuality debate will be their primary battleground.

✚ The liberal single-issue groups are likely to decline in influence and resources to undertake their mission.

✚ Conservative lobbying groups will in turn become increasingly powerful, having the funds and sophistication to run influential campaigns.

✚ The Church in general will move toward the center under the pressure of conservative groups.

✚ The conservative single-issue groups will give increasing attention to their perception that Christian orthodoxy is now under attack.

CHAPTER THIRTEEN

The Rise of Networks, the Decline of Hierarchy

Throughout America, it looks very much as if hierarchies are going the way of the dinosaur. Whether you're on Wall Street, Main Street, or Factory Row, as restructuring takes place, pyramids of authority are being flattened out or are even disappearing altogether. They are being replaced by networks, which in turn are forming all sorts of creative linkages between clusters of people with shared interests who are focused on a particular goal. Put another way, authority structures are giving way to relationship structures.

As each day passes we move irrevocably further from the familiar ordering of society we had grown used to in the forty years following World War II. Although the reasons for this metamorphosis are complex, behind it are both generational and technological changes. In addition, they reflect the undisputed fact that the kind of hierarchy that shaped America's life during the period when it was rising to world power no longer work as effectively as they once did.

The authors of *Megatrends 2000* put it this way:

> The failure of hierarchies to solve society's problems forced people to talk to one another—and that was the

> beginning of networks....Simply stated, networks are
> people talking to each other, sharing ideas, information
> and resources....The important part is not the network, the
> finished product, but the process of getting there—the com-
> munication that creates the linkages between people and
> clusters of people....Networks exist to foster self-help, to ex-
> change information, to change society, to improve produc-
> tivity,...and to share resources."[1]

Almost everywhere, in the non-profit sector as well as in business, networks are rapidly becoming the norm. Whether we like it or not, as the transition to an "information society" further accelerates, the hierarchies in western culture that remain will crumble or disappear. We are likely to see them replaced by a multiplicity of networks. While there are many Episcopalians who probably wish the Information Age would go away, we are only at the very beginning of a communications convulsion that will challenge most of our dearly cherished organizational presuppositions.

Perhaps because they have been conditioned by centuries of hierarchical ordering, churches seem to find it particularly difficult to digest the implications of all that is happening, and to adjust their denominational structures accordingly. Despite the Body of Christ imagery Scripture uses to describe the Church, imagery that is implicitly organic rather than hierarchical, generations of pyramid-style authority structures do not disappear overnight. Regardless of the Church's attachment to hierarchies, we have no doubt their days are numbered. The time has come for them to be radically reshaped.

A New Generation

A primary reason for the demise of present structures is the retirement and passing on of the torch of leadership by the generation that grew to adulthood during the Great

Depression and World War II. They were teamworkers, who flourished when given "strong" leadership, and although the cohort that followed them has tried (with diminishing success) to sustain the structures received from their elders, we cannot expect them to remain intact as leadership now begins to pass into the hands of baby boomers.[2]

The latter, who came to adulthood in the 1960s and early 1970s, grew up with the assumption that no leader is above reproof, and that all leaders should be kept under constant scrutiny. After all, this is the crowd who once thought no one over the age of thirty could be trusted!

While leadership might be passing into their hands, they still suspect hierarchies, and there is a subconscious distrust of those in authority—even their own peers. They want power bases to be broad, lines of authority short, and they expect a high degree of accountability. Networks suit their modus vivendi admirably. We would be fooling ourselves if we thought the Episcopal Church could escape their scrutiny. Wherever they stand on the religious or political spectrum, we can expect Episcopalians of this generation to retool the Church in line with these preferences.

The boomer generation is now being elected to positions of responsibility in the Episcopal Church, a fact confirmed by a mere glance at the ages of some of the recently consecrated bishops, seminary deans, and cardinal rectors. While there might not be as many of them active in the Church's life as were baptized into its fellowship, this generation has totally redefined society with each chapter of its development. In the Episcopal Church, their reach is likely to far exceed their numbers.

The Church they are inheriting was constructed by a 100% male leadership, much more at home with hierarchy and military-style command structures than today's people. Since the time of Bishop Henry Knox Sherrill, the nature of leadership has been defined by those who fought on the Normandy beaches, in the Pacific, or in Korea. The structures with which they were comfortable were then fine-tuned to be in harmony with the 1950s and 1960s configurations of American business and industry. The Presiding Bishop's position was shaped in such a way that he became the religious equivalent of CEO of a nationwide organization. He is the one of the few primates in the Anglican Communion without diocesan jurisdiction, a position now contrary to the 1988 recommendations of the Lambeth Conference of Bishops.

The rising generation of Episcopal leaders are not likely to be comfortable with these inherited styles. They are men and women who protested a war rather than fighting one. It is also likely they are less comfortable than their predecessors with the trappings of corporate America, and much more willing to experiment. Boomers are getting set to retool every organization in America according to their own priorities and values, and we cannot expect the Episcopal Church to escape from their scrutiny.

To this generation networking comes naturally. They get impatient with unwieldy, inflexible organizations that are not designed to listen and respond to the grass roots. These Episcopalians are more likely to feel that if they cannot have "hands on" involvement then they are not interested in being involved at all. Failure to reform Episcopal Church structures would not only straightjacket the Church and trap it in a bygone age, but it could also rob us of significant leadership talent.

Changing Structures, Voluntary Agencies, and the National Church

But there is another side to the present configurations that ought to give us pause for thought. Not too long ago, writing to the editor of *The Living Church*, James L. Duncan, retired Bishop of Southeast Florida, wrote that before World War II,

> the diocese and the national church vocation was to assist parishes in their ministry....Today, the diocese and the national church's approach is that the parish exists to carry on the diocesan and national programs rather than to strengthen and make effective the parish.[3]

Bishop Duncan sees the origins of this trend in the 1960s, when the Church sought to face the challenge of systemic evils that pervaded society. While we affirm that this tendency reached its full flowering in the 1960s, it has a much longer history and was simply reinforced by the agenda of that stormy period.

As these questions are raised within the Episcopal Church, there is parallel discontent with denominational structures in other churches struggling with national frameworks not unlike our own, and constructed during the same era.

A leading Presbyterian academic, John Mulder, commenting on a parallel trend within the Presbyterian Church (USA), suggests we should be surprised not that centralized denominational leadership is weakening, but that it managed to survive for so long. He observes that our present configurations were put into place in the first part of this century to facilitate mission. Over the years they have been turned from enablers into regulatory bodies, and now tend to work at cross-purposes with the mission of the local congregations they were designed to serve.

Whether the denominational structure is Presbyterian, Methodist, or Episcopal, all seem to have either overlooked or forgotten that the primary unit of ministry is neither the diocese nor the national church, but the individual congregation. In his keynote address to the Province VII

Stewardship Conference in 1990, Bishop William G. Burrill said:

> For a long time, without consciously talking about it we thought parishes existed to support the diocese and that the diocese existed to support the national church. The fact of the matter is, the dioceses and the national church only exist to support the local congregations. The question is, does the structure of the national church and any particular diocese basically serve the local church?

Although these statements certainly are at odds with the traditional Anglican teaching that the diocese is the basic unit of church life, a strong streak of congregationalism runs through Episcopal Church history, and the reality has usually been that the diocese is only as strong as its ability to serve and provide resources for its parishes.

We do not believe it coincidental that in the 1960s, just as the hierarchical top-down structure functioning out of the brand-new corporate headquarters building at 815 Second Avenue, New York, reached its zenith, small voluntary agencies also began to mushroom. The seeds of dissatisfaction with the Episcopal Church Center were most likely sown by the divisiveness of the General Convention Special Budget, the Church's attempt to respond to the urban crisis that swept the USA in the late 1960s. Since then, these new organizations have challenged centralized structures, and when those structures have not responded, they have often ignored them and simply continued their own alternative ministries.

Able to respond to both real and felt needs, many of these agencies have the flexibility to respond to changing circumstances in ways the national church, tied as it is to a triennial General Convention, cannot. Indeed, many of the smaller agencies can turn on a dime. Both when circumstances demand a new direction or when funding is difficult, they are able to reorder their priorities with rapidity and precision. Furthermore, many of the newer agencies represent theologically and politically conservative positions that have been out of favor in the liberal environment of the formal leadership structures.

This expanding network of intentional agencies, each with a clear focus and precisely stated mission, is in the process of changing the face of the Church. As if to emphasize their independence from the national structures, their offices are seldom found in the New York metropolitan area, but are often located near one of the various regional centers of influence in the Episcopal Church: Sewanee, Tennessee; Kanuga in North Carolina; Northern Virginia; and now in increasing numbers, Ambridge, Pennsylvania. This diaspora further illustrates the movement away from a centralized hierarchy to an interconnected series of networks with multiple foci.

There is often a high degree of cooperation among these various associations with related agendas, but neither should we ignore the concomitant competition—especially for funds. But relevant units for the Episcopal Church Center can no longer predominate and set the agenda, as they might have done in the past. In today's climate they are expected to function as equal partners with the others in the natural democracy of these networks.

An example of these interrelated networks is the Episcopal Council for Global Mission. It is consciously patterned after the Council for Women's Ministries. Maybe it is significant that the most effective networking styles have been pioneered by women and that they are now being shared by a broader cross-section of organizations. This is, perhaps, evidence that the writing could well be on the wall for the "power" assumptions of a more masculine ilk that are built into traditional, hierarchical styles of organization.

As we see greater male/female partnership, we should not be surprised that the emphasis on nurturing so important in feminine relationships is beginning to assert itself in networking styles, and in the management of Church life. We should be excited that organizational patterns are developing that make us seriously consider what it means to be the Body of Christ. This is healthy and should encourage us as we explore various new ways of organizing ourselves.

Despite the inherent difficulty in a host of small agencies struggling to make ends meet and accomplish their mission, this style of life seems functional in today's Church, where networks are becoming the norm and extremely high levels of accountability are demanded. While some of these agencies will inevitably fall by the wayside, we can expect others to reach increasing levels of maturity during the coming decade, and to be playing a significant role as the twenty-first century dawns.

The apparent indecisiveness of the 70th General Convention in Phoenix, Arizona, in 1991, and the perception that the House of Bishops is unable to provide leadership and a sense of direction, will lead to the further strengthening of these voluntary organizations. We are certain there will be the establishment of new agencies to fill the vacuum left by present leadership patterns. This multiplication of independent entities is itself an example of the continuing fragmentation of received national church structures.

A Different Kind of Leadership

Managing a multiplicity of organizations and networks will require highly developed negotiating and listening skills among our leaders. Indeed, it will require a very different style of leadership altogether, one prepared to facilitate a new vision of what the Episcopal Church is called to be, and mediate disputes when radical disagreements inevitably erupt. We believe it vital that those in leadership make peace with, rather than deny, these changing patterns that promise liberation from past errors. To ignore what is happening could imperil the healthy development of the Church as we move into a new century.[4]

As networks continue to emerge, the Executive Council, Episcopal Church Center, and General Convention will find it increasingly difficult to make strategic decisions without both taking them into account, and including them in the decision-making process. Their exclusion from participation in the formal debates shaping the life of the Church is already spawning deep alienation and, in effect, setting up a church within the Church. Perhaps the starkest example of this has been the development of the Episcopal Synod of America, which believes its concerns are neither heard nor acknowledged.

And New Kinds of Structures...

We believe a majority of Episcopalians genuinely wish to cooperate with the Episcopal Church Center at 815 Second Avenue, New York, and with the national leadership of the Church. However, in the coming decade we expect there will be increasing and persistent calls for a radical overhaul of the system. These began in earnest at the 1991 General Convention, with the call by both bishops and deputies for an administrative review of the Church's structure, operation, and program. For procedural reasons, when re-presented the resolution failed, but the writing is on the wall.[5]

In many ways, the Church Center has been the White House of the Episcopal Church, but in the eyes of many it has also turned itself into an expensive White Elephant. In Phoenix, the General Convention once again gave permission for another study concerning the possible relocation of the Episcopal Church Center away from New York City.

This transition from hierarchies to networks raises complex questions about its nature, location, and structure. Although many balked at the idea of moving from New York in the mid-1980s, you can be certain that voices raised in the 1990s will come up with more radical and even iconoclastic solutions to this problem.

To those at the conservative end of the church's theological and social continuum, the Episcopal Church Center is seen to be "a bastion of arrogant liberalism." They are infuriated by its apparently unflinching commitment to an agenda they believe is at odds with the vast majority of Episcopalians in the pews. To Episcopalians of this shade, it has no credibility, and they perceive that it is determined to withstand change, ignoring Christian sanity. On the other hand, to huge numbers of Episcopalians, the Church Center is more of an irritating irrelevance than an enemy. Stances taken and decisions made within its walls are greeted with yawns and widely ignored by many as they get on with their own business.

Both of us have traveled widely around the Church since the mid-1980s. Prior to that time, criticism of the national church was considered "unpatriotic" and in extremely poor taste. Yet wherever we go today, the reverse is the case. Almost everywhere, it has become fashionable to say at least one bad word about it. This reversal is a demonstration that, one way or another, major changes will be forced upon the national church in the coming years.

We suspect attempts to do more than tinker with present structures will be strenuously opposed by many on the Executive Council, those appointed to the Church's interim bodies, as well as those whose jobs would be threatened by radical changes involving the Episcopal Church Center. Eventually pressure of circumstances and a cacophony of voices, however, will force this issue onto the table for debate. Demographics alone demonstrate that New York is no longer the center of gravity of the Episcopal Church; this has moved to the more conservative Sun Belt states.

The growing trend toward non-payment of assessments to the national church budget is not just due to parishes withholding support from their dioceses, but may also be the first symptom of other, general pressures being brought to bear through the Church. Money, of course, speaks louder than words. Perhaps we are seeing baby boomers and their allies flexing their muscles. Are they using the targeted withholding of funds to encourage the Church to change? They are certainly a generation who understand the meaning of "value added." Nothing is sacred in their eyes, and whatever does not deliver back the initial investment put into it should be axed.

Maybe fiscal restraints are the only way the Episcopal Church can be forced to adapt to the extraordinary sea changes that are taking place all round us. Should restructuring come as a result of a budget crisis, it is our fear that it will be perceived as a failure rather than as an exciting opportunity to extend our mission in visionary and less restricted ways. If this is the case, mixed signals will be sent out from "the top."

Changes in our society and the manner in which we organize ourselves are also accelerating the time when the General Convention itself will come under scrutiny. Recently the rector of Trinity Church, Wall Street, remarked:

> The timing and structure of the General Convention were established two hundred years ago. Intervals of three years were not unreasonable in the pace of those times, not to mention the limits of travel. For instance, what business person today can take three weeks out to attend the General Convention? Is it any wonder that the leadership of the Church is gravitating into the hands of church professionals?[6]

Its unwieldy size, the long intervals between meetings, and the inability of a body of 1,500 people to respond with rapidity and flexibility are issues that must be discussed. Add to that the colossal expense of such an undertaking, and it is clear the time has come for radical changes to be made. What changes could be wrought if half the funds spent by the national church, dioceses, exhibitors, and individual visitors were spent instead on spreading the Gospel, housing the homeless, and bringing relief to those living with AIDS!

As the Convention comes under scrutiny, proposals both reasonable and ridiculous will be made. It is our estimate that intensifying and persistent demands for decentralization will become louder. These will be linked to ideas for the strengthening of the nine provinces of the Church, a significant reduction of delegates to future Conventions, and the possible scheduling of meetings at intervals of twelve to eighteen months.

If such reordering takes place, then we can expect a fierce debate to erupt about the function and role of future Presiding Bishops. The Presiding Bishop has an almost impossible job description, one that is beyond the ability of any man or woman to fulfill. Since its primary task is that of shepherd and pastor to the other bishops of the Church, perhaps the office of Presiding Bishop should be separated from the administration of both program and budget, while maintaining oversight through chairing the Executive Council. This would remove from the Presiding Bishop's job description an impossible load of administrative functions, thus freeing the time to exercise the primary task of the *episcope* of the whole Church.

There are no easy answers. Growing evidence suggests that Episcopalians are eager to see changes in ecclesiastical structures. Yet as this takes place, we are forced to ask "What is really the task of the Church?" With the debate heating up during the 1990s we will be expected to decide whether present structures help or hinder the ministry of the Church.

And if the national church comes under scrutiny, so will the dioceses. During the last fifteen years, it has become increasingly difficult for dioceses without a significant endowment to make ends meet. Numerical decline and rising overheads have forced painful downsizing on many. Many dioceses still find it difficult to accept the reality that the basic unit of American church life—Anglican ecclesiology aside—is the congregation and not the diocese. Those dioceses that cling to the old hierarchical pattern are the ones having the most difficult time.

If the next ten years are likely to see Episcopalians asking questions about the national shape of the Church, dioceses will come under the microscope too. Questions like, "What is a viable diocese?" "Are some dioceses too large?" "Do we have too many?" will abound. Then it will be asked if they are absorbing too many valuable assets and delivering too little in the way of services back to the parishes. Against such a utilitarian backdrop, it is not only the Presiding Bishop who will have his job description radically rewritten. At this very moment, the House of Bishops is in the midst of the preparation of a pastoral letter examining the role and ministry of a bishop, which in turn is likely to affect the job descriptions of the bishops who write it.

Times of change bring great opportunities. The transition from hierarchies to networks will surely bring about many of the most immediately observable changes in the life of the Episcopal Church. While these will not be easy years for the organizational structures of the Church, we can expect them to yield opportunities of mission and ministry that can only be the doing of the Holy Spirit. Whether we respond to the

Spirit's prompting, or conveniently turn the other way, is the question Episcopalians must now ask of themselves.

TRENDS TO WATCH

✚ We will see a radical shift from a centralized national church structure to one based on networks.

✚ The parishes, instead of the national church or dioceses, will be regarded as the primary units of mission.

✚ This transition will be accompanied and encouraged by the targeted use of funds. Money will become an increasingly attractive way for the grass-roots organizations to express their opinions.

✚ There will be a continued multiplication of voluntary agencies in the life of the Church.

✚ As baby boomers, especially women, increasingly take leadership in the life of the Church, they will change its operating patterns to suit their own preferences.

CHAPTER FOURTEEN

Episcopalians As World Christians

When it was first made public, Marshall McLuhan's idea seemed so far-fetched. "One day there will be a kind of global village," the Canadian communications guru predicted in the 1960s, and many of the wise sagely shook their heads. But McLuhan was right, and today we are grappling to come to terms with his future now that is our present.

On January 16, 1991, we watched with a mixture of fascination and horror as three CNN reporters lay on the floor of a hotel room and provided a running commentary on the pictures being beamed to our TV screens of the first wave of Allied air attacks on Bagdad. Never before in human history had it been possible to watch a war from behind enemy lines while it was actually being fought. If ever we needed proof of the global village, this was it.

More than TV news has been internationalized. Today we drive cars design and built in half a dozen different countries and work for multinational corporations. We can talk to friends and family on the other side of the world by just lifting the receiver and punching in a handful of numbers, and we can be there in a day if a crisis occurs. While modern transportation has brought the whole planet to our doorstep, telephones, TV, radio, computer networks, and satellites provide the communications linkages vital to everyday life. Adapting to these changed circumstances can be traumatic, but it is not an option we can ignore. Now and in the future all markets are global—as are all economic, military, ethical, ecological, and religious issues.

To date, the Episcopal Church has only half-digested the implications of globalization. We are proud to be part of the worldwide Anglican Communion, but we have yet to discover the exciting side of this equation: what it means to be world Christians. Our legislative bodies spend a great deal of time on a selection of international issues, such as peace in Central America, or justice in South Africa, but our membership is oblivious to and lacks curiosity about the radical implications of sharing the Gospel in this increasingly interdependent world. We will talk for hours about responding to the urban crisis at home, but are both silent and ignorant about the almost impossible task of evangelism and compassionate ministry facing Christians in Shanghai, Mexico City, or Sao Paulo, where the population is over twenty million and climbing.

By coupling the transportation and telecommunications revolution with the extraordinary growth of Christianity in the last one hundred years, for the first time in history it is possible to talk meaningfully of ours as a truly global faith. Although this may represent a reality that is unpalatable to most Episcopalians, Christian initiative has now passed from western hands, and today is in the hands of our sisters and brothers in the Two-Thirds World. As the truth dawns, it could be a painful awakening for many of us.

A Plurality of Religions

In early January, Richard Kew was riding a commuter train from the suburbs into the center of London, in order to spend a day working and consulting with colleagues at the

British headquarters of SPCK. So that no time would be wasted when he reached the office, he was refreshing his memory from a file of papers he had brought with him. In the Middle East, two great armies were lined up against one another, and it was popularly, but falsely, perceived that the forthcoming battle would be between "Christian" nations and a Moslem tyrant.

As Kew glanced out of the window, he noticed that the kind-faced man sitting next to him was also working on a pile of documents. While his fellow passenger was on his way to the annual meeting of an Islamic mission agency, intent on reaching the world with the message of the Prophet, Kew's papers focused on the task of proclaiming Christ worldwide.

This encounter illustrates how the religions of the world are jumbled together as never before. However unstable it has been at times, the old religious consensus in America of Protestants, Catholics, and Jews is now giving way to new players. Immigration, intermarriage, and conversion have brought Hindus, Buddhists, and Moslems into our population in increasing numbers, not to mention the growth of quasi-Christian sects like the Mormons, and eastern groups like the Unification Church and the whole New Age movement.

How are we all to live together is a question we will be asking with increasing frequency in coming years. By 2020, Judaism will have been eclipsed by Islam as America's second largest religion. We have yet seriously to explore the implications of Islam's growth. How many young men and women will be drawn into organizations like Louis Farrakhan's Nation of Islam by urban despair, drug abuse, and economic hardship? (We must not forget that Farrakhan himself grew up in the Episcopal Church and was an acolyte at Christ Church, Roxbury, Massachusetts before renouncing Christianity for Islam.) As Atef A. Gawad writes,

> Islam is not only a faith. It is a complete way of life, an articulate platform for political action, and a vigorous program for ordering society. The prophet Mohammed founded not only a community, but also a polity, a sovereign state, and an empire.[1]

Islam cannot be ignored, and neither is it going to go away. At home and abroad, it could be the greatest challenge facing the Christian Church during the coming century. Whether in the streets of Harlem, the cities of the Middle East, or in Sub-Saharan Africa, where Christianity and Islam meet, a head-on confrontation is not going to solve problems. We must not blindly turn our backs on this great faith with its rich heritage of art, poetry, and science, but we must apply our minds and imaginations to responding to its challenge without compromising our commitment to Christ.

Christians who are students of the world's religions have learned to respect and honor their many helpful spiritual insights, but in so doing they have often minimized Christian claims and demands. Some have reacted against the arrogance, colonialism, and pretended superiority that have sometimes colored facets of Christian missions. The result has been a "democratization" of religious claims that can lead to a denigration of some of the fundamental beliefs of their own faith. In doing so they have fallen backwards into another form of arrogance, obscuring the magnificent truths implicit and explicit in Christ's crucified love. Therefore, one of the greatest global challenges will be to discover how we can have healthy and open-ended dialogue with other faiths without compromising the uniqueness of the claims of Christ. In this, we suspect we will learn from Two-Thirds World Christians who, unlike ourselves, do not have a history of imperialism that unwittingly becomes entangled with our theological reflection.

The Rise of the Two-Thirds World Church

An intriguing global reality is that just as the West is consolidating its political power throughout the world following the collapse of the Eastern bloc, the transfer of spiritual power to the non-western world is well underway. Indeed, for the Christian faith we have already passed a point of virtual no return.

In many respects, the Anglican Communion is further down the road in its transition of leadership from the First to the Two-Thirds World than most other Christian traditions. During the last two centuries of mission, Anglicans have established churches that are now almost all nationally autonomous. Our polity has left their bishops and people with an independence to develop an appropriate style and agenda that properly reflects their own culture. Significant maturation has occurred in many of these places, so today expatriate bishops have disappeared from all but the most missionary of Anglican dioceses. Even in these places their days are numbered.

The 1988 Lambeth Conference was where the torch of leadership symbolically passed from the British Isles and North America to Africa. Two observers have written, "The Africans cut confident figures, coming from churches that are growing and have a strong voice in the councils of the nation."[2] Afterward, Kenya's Bishop David Gitari declared that anyone wanting to shape the life of the Communion through the episcopate at the Lambeth Conference in 1998 will first have to square their proposals with the largest and most powerful bloc of bishops—the Africans.

While in the American Church we might rejoice heartily if a diocese planted a new congregation every four or five years, in many parts of the world evangelism and church growth are enabling dioceses to establish two or three congregations a month. In 1990, the Church of Nigeria, one of the largest provinces in the Anglican Communion with at least a million members more than the Episcopal Church, consecrated eight missionary bishops to establish new dioceses in the northern part of that country. Much as the demolition of the Berlin Wall, the liberation of Central Europe, and the collapse of the Communist Party in the former Soviet Union are revamping international politics, during the 1990s we will have to learn to relate to our global partners in radically different ways.

The 1990s will see most of the vestiges of religious leadership pass from European and North American hands. The cutting edge of theology, Christian ethics, evangelism, and mission is rapidly moving to the global "South." The primary asset that remains to us in the western churches is financial wealth. If we are tempted to use our relative affluence to manipulate these burgeoning churches, especially during the 1990s when new patterns of relationship are being forged, a breakdown of trust could occur that would do great damage to the Gospel.

"Adjusting to the internationalization of the Gospel is a very difficult process," writes the former editor of *World Christian* magazine. We find ourselves face-to-face with "new faces, strange names, different theological concepts, a rainbow of colors," and we are no longer the head of the family. We must listen to and learn from them in the 1990s, and "make it our pattern to defer to non-western opinions and ideas whenever our most basic convictions are not at stake."[3]

What makes learning more difficult for many Americans is that the theological and spiritual priorities of the worldwide Anglican Communion are very different from the North American Episcopal tradition. Predominantly evangelical, with a strong and growing charismatic wing, the Anglican Communion as a whole has little patience with much of our theologizing and our subjective attitudes toward morality. One example of this is the issue of homosexual rights. At the 1988 Lambeth Conference, Bishop Paul Moore of New York argued that homosexual tendencies were a result of a chemical imbalance in the body and therefore not a subject for praise or blame. Demanding that Scripture cannot be divorced from behavior and must be read in relation to ethical imperatives, Archbishop Manasses Kuria of Kenya answered him by saying, "Homosexuals have rights as human beings. But they do not have rights as homosexuals. Homosexuality is sin. We do not call homosexuals to be faithful in marriage to one another."[4]

A New Tribalism and A "New World Order"

In *Megatrends 2000,* John Naisbitt and Patricia Aburdene Morrow start their chapter, "Global Lifestyles and Cultural Nationalism," with the following words:

> Today, thanks to a thriving world economy, global telecommunications, and expanding travel, exchange among Europe, North America, and the Pacific Rim is happening at an unparalleled pace. In the urban centers of the developing world signs of the international youth culture are almost everywhere. So enthusiastically are we swapping food, music, and fashion that a new international lifestyle reigns in Osaka, Madrid, and Seattle....But even as our lifestyles grow more similar, there are unmistakable signs of a powerful countertrend: a backlash against uniformity, a desire to assert the uniqueness of one's culture and language, a repudiation of foreign influence.[5]

During the next decade we can expect to see a wholesale redrawing of the world map. National boundaries will look very different when the new century begins, as ethnic groups seek independence and dignity, and new regional consortia are formed. With the Cold War over and the political verities of that period obliterated, we must expect greater, rather than reduced, instability. Simmering tribalism in Central Europe and the Balkans, the aftermath of the break-up of the Soviet Union, the plight of the Kurds, and the changing face of Africa are all bound to affect international relationships and impinge on our global ministry. While smaller racial groups are being reshaped, larger political alliances are being forged to enable trade and mutual defense. It could be that we are seeing the beginning of the demise of the nation-state as we have known it. We can expect to see terrorism and open warfare as ethnic groups attempt to challenge national sovereignties, with the US and other western governments puzzled about how to respond appropriately to such yearnings for liberty.

We are not in the business of gazing into crystal balls to foretell the future, but after forty years of standoff, the world is a political and social melting-pot. Yet there seems to be little debate within the Episcopal Church about the impact this "new world order" (whatever that means!) will have upon us, and the manner in which we will function internationally. While political change has brought to the surface antagonisms between ethnic groups and their governments, it is also the harbinger of spiritual awakenings. Reports from China suggest continued church growth, despite the crackdown in Tiananmen Square. We have seen extraordinary new things happening in the Russian Church, and there are reports of an openness to Christianity in some of the eastern republics of what was the Soviet Union. Meanwhile a growing ferment among the formerly suppressed churches of Eastern Europe will not leave us untouched.

Discernment and grace will be required of us as we weave our way through the changing landscape. We will be looked to for assistance, as well as given occasional lectures about our self-contented affluence. At this crucial moment in history, we believe the Episcopal Church has a role to play. We are being asked not only to redouble our missionary effort, but also to undertake our global ministry with a new humility, imagination, and God-given creativity. We will play our role badly if we do not quickly open the debate among ourselves, and also sink to our knees in prayer.

Challenge of Pluralism

America contains the greatest diaspora of nations of all time! The languages of over 90% of the world's population are the first tongues of many American residents, and the plurality of religions and customs is extraordinary. Everywhere round the world, technological advances, coupled with war, famine, persecution, and the eagerness for opportunity, have made people more mobile than any time in human history. In some cases, we do not have to go out into all the world to find its peoples, for they are coming to us, settling here as a result of either voluntary or forced emigration from their homelands. Addressing a meeting of the Executive Council of the Episcopal Church in June 1990, the Bishop of San Joaquin was forthright in his assertion that we must expand our ministry among the ethnic groups flooding in.

This might seem a tall order given our limited success to date with the most significant ethnic minority to have entered in large numbers, the Hispanics. However, with the Anglo proportion of the population rapidly declining, we have no option but to reach out at home or we will quickly turn into a minority ethnic church in our own right.

The need to structure ourselves for mission among diverse and growing ethnic groups has been further endorsed by priests of ethnic minority backgrounds in the

Church. For example, Duc X. Nguyen, vicar of the Church of the Redeemer, Garden Grove, California, a Vietnamese congregation, has disturbing questions about our approach toward incoming minorities. He wonders why the Episcopal Church does as much, if not more, than many other traditions to meet the *social* needs of immigrants and refugees, but then keeps its mouth firmly shut when it comes to telling them about Christ.

The presence of so many immigrants gives many of our parishes the opportunity for cross-cultural ministry. Few are in a position to develop an outreach mission like the Church of the Holy Comforter, Vienna, Virginia, which now undertakes ministry among the Urdu-speaking Pakistani population of the Washington, D.C., area. But even in the small towns of rural America it is now possible to find a small community of Japanese business people, Filipinos whose spouses met and married them when on active military service, or seasonal farm workers from Mexico, Guatemala, or Honduras. These people have great social and spiritual needs, and the 1990s give Episcopal parishes the chance to share Christ with them.

But migration is a two-way street. While returning from Uruguay recently, Richard Kew found himself sitting on a plane beside an American married to a Uruguayan, who chooses to live in that country rather than in the United States. Then there are diplomats, teachers, and businesspeople who ply their trade around the world—many of whom are Episcopalians. Numbers of these people have work that takes them into countries where missionaries cannot go.

While there might be limitations on the way in which they can witness to their faith, in the 1990s we should be providing training, as the Episcopal Church did in the 1960s, for them to "be" Christ in the places to which they go. These "passport missionaries" may be enabled to undertake acts of love and plant seeds of faith that will grow and flourish in the years after their return home.

Learning to Think and Act Globally

The slogan "Think globally, act locally" has been around for years, but it has made a limited impact on Episcopalians when it comes to our approach to mission and ministry. Our tendency is to think and act locally. Somehow or other we lost our global vision during the 1950s and 1960s, and it is only slowly returning. During the 1990s, whether Episcopalians like it or not, this is going to be an item moving up the Church's agenda, for with each passing day the culture in which we live is becoming ever more global. Yet this is not a fact taken seriously by our seminaries.

The Association of Theological Schools, the regulatory body of North American theological education, has called on all its members to "globalize" their teaching and curriculum, but Episcopal schools have been slow to respond. While representatives of the seminaries are involving themselves with peers at gatherings in Asia, Africa, and Latin America, this has not yet affected style or content of teaching. Moreover, the breadth of theology from the Two-Thirds World is not taken seriously by most Episcopal seminary professors, either. Although there is a fascination with liberation theology from Latin America, little consideration is given to the creative work being undertaken by Christians on other continents.[6]

However, it is encouraging to see some seminaries regaining lost ground. In 1988, Virginia Theological Seminary, once the pioneer in global ministry education, appointed its first Professor of World Mission for a generation. Two years later, Trinity Episcopal School for Ministry established the Stanway Institute of Evangelism and World Mission in memory of the founding president of the seminary. More recently, a global ministry program has been established and funded at Episcopal Divinity School, Cambridge, Massachusetts. We believe this recovery of the global focus in theological education will accelerate as the 1990s proceed.

Such a recovery will require much painful rethinking. Across the Communion there are constant calls that we move away from the pastoral model of parish ministry that was appropriate when most people lived in compact, intimate rural communities, toward a mission model that reaches out in Christ's name beyond the immediate congregation. In North America, the pastoral model of ministry continues to reign supreme, and most of our theological educators lack the courage to pick up the mission ball. We have before us ten or fifteen fascinating years when globalization is going to reshape radically the whole field of theological education! Is the Episcopal Church going to be left behind or not?

New Patterns of Global Engagement

Until the 1970s, virtually all global mission ministry in the Episcopal Church was focused around the World Mission Unit at the Episcopal Church Center. During the 1970s and 1980s a series of voluntary societies came into being, which forced the Church to rethink its approach to involvement in global mission. While they were not the first voluntary agencies in the modern era in the Church, their focus and function have proved transformational. The Overseas Mission Society of the 1960s was the first voluntary agency, but it was set up more as an enabler and think-tank, than as an actual practitioner of global ministry.

During the 1990s we are beginning to see these independent agencies come to maturity, increasingly sharing the responsibility for world mission with the World Mission

Unit. While it might be fair to describe the latter as the "State Department" of the Church as it relates to overseas Christians, the voluntary societies undertake specific tasks providing prayer, human resources, literature, and education materials, for example. The largest of these is the South American Missionary Society. Founded in 1976, it is hoping to see the number of personnel deployed in Latin America rise from twenty-five to forty by the end of 1992. Their particular commitment is to evangelism, church planting, health care, and education in their target countries. It does all this on an income of little more than $900,000 per year. The missionaries of SAMS travel around the Church seeking support, and have played a significant role in raising the Episcopal Church's world mission profile.

The oldest voluntary society is the Episcopal Church Missionary Community. Through the vision of Walter and Louise Hannum, ECMC has connected our Church to the activities that have developed from the seminal world mission thinking at Fuller Seminary in Pasadena, California. Such activities have oriented missionaries for service, and encouraged prayer and education about the global task. Having recently relocated to Ambridge, Pennsylvania, the Hannums are now involved in the development of the Stanway Institute for Evangelism and World Mission at Trinity Episcopal School for Ministry.

The Society for Promoting Christian Knowledge, the oldest mission agency in Anglicanism, was established here in 1983 and provides resources for feeding hungry minds. SPCK/USA today works in forty-two countries, has provided considerable numbers of books for seminary libraries, and undertakes the development of Spanish language resources. This society is seeking to expand education resources to enable Episcopalians to better understand world mission. In an Information Age there is a need for an information mission agency.

Other agencies include the Episcopal World Mission, Sharing of Ministries Abroad (SOMA), Christian Ministry Among Jewish People (CMJ), and the Church Army. Even more controversial are efforts to establish another agency to share the Gospel with those who have never heard it, an Anglican Frontier Mission, which will surely heighten conflict between theological evangelicals and liberals in the field of world mission. We can expect it to spawn a considerable debate about the ecumenicity of world religions, the uniqueness of God's revelation in Jesus Christ, and theological pluralism within the mission of the Church.

Most of these organizations belong to the Episcopal Council for Global Mission, and attempt to cooperate with one another, coordinating work wherever possible. The growth of the independent agencies has been extraordinary during the past two decades, and as they continue to expand during this decade, they are bound to influence the Church's understanding of its international responsibilities, as well as the manner in which it undertakes them. Although they seek to work within communion-wide guidelines, these agencies have the flexibility and freedom to respond to changing circumstances. Slowed down by the inevitable constitutional limitations imposed by the Executive Council and General Convention, the World Mission Unit lacks the ability to respond speedily to new challenges and opportunities. Yet each agency needs the other, and during the 1990s we can look to see an interesting symbiosis of mission developing.

Our World Mission Future

The Episcopal Church was once one of the leaders in world mission. Today the global consciousness of the Episcopal Church is beginning to stir once more. Out of the present ferment will come new patterns of mission and ministry. With the world in such a fluid state, and with a significant theological transition occurring in the life of the Church, we can expect considerable conflict to surround the area of world mission in coming years.

We have hidden for too long behind the platitude that all Episcopalians are missionaries simply because they are members of the Domestic and Foreign Missionary Society, the formal name under which the Episcopal Church is incorporated. In the light of the theology of the Baptismal Covenant, the time is long overdue to turn this platitude into a reality by living out the directive "to proclaim the Gospel in word and deed" in the global village.

However, this will be an exciting decade. We fully expect to see today's vast global changes stimulating greater interest in our mission in the world, and the changing structures of world mission within the Episcopal Church are likely to encourage this. The pieces are starting to fall into place, and we believe that we should be planning now for our approach to the global task during the first decade of the twenty-first century.

TRENDS TO WATCH

✚ The Episcopal Church will begin to wrestle seriously with the implications of "the global village," although it will be difficult for the Episcopal Church to learn to defer to non-western views and opinions.

✚ As the power shift from the western churches to those in the Two-Thirds World continues, we expect to see the Episcopal Church give increasing attention to the way this will affect our life.

✚ Despite the challenge, we do not expect the Episcopal Church to make significant headway among the increasing number of ethnic minorities within the United States.

✚ The seminaries will begin to address the opportunities of "the internationalization of theology."

✚ There will be continued growth in the voluntary mission agencies and a radical restructuring of the way we undertake global mission as a Church.

CHAPTER FIFTEEN

Where Are the Trends Taking Us?

W hen we began this attempt to identify the trends shaping the future of our Church, we noticed that what is happening in the Episcopal Church has a clear parallel in the other mainstream churches in this country. Like it or not, we are all perceived to be in difficulty. If we were to look at these difficulties on their own, they could discourage us terribly; however, after digesting the information we have presented between the covers of this book, it is obvious there are plenty of rays of light slanting into the life of our Church. Yet the time is long overdue for us to address some of the less pleasant realities that continue to haunt us. We have reached a critical chapter change in our history, and we are being asked to undertake some radical rethinking of our place in society and the way we should function.

But there are other realities. Each section of this book is designed to demonstrate that the trends shaping our future have within them clues that can hearten us as we gaze toward the distant horizon. We are unapologetic when we say that our study of these trends makes us both enthusiastic and optimistic about what lies ahead for the life of the Episcopal Church. So often seeds of hope begin to sprout even as the bad news is being proclaimed—it was true for the

Apostles, it is true for us today. This bad news has helped us understand the lay of the land. We are now in a position to refocus, re-form ourselves, and redirect our energies. There is a biblical principle: after death comes resurrection.

The systemic changes we are called upon to make may be painful. Inevitably we will be asked to give up facets of Episcopal Church life that we prize, but that for the majority are neither relevant nor any longer appropriate. It is never easy to lay aside things that have become familiar or are particularly precious to us. But what we love may not necessarily be helpful to the future life of the Episcopal Church. This is part of the "little death" that heralds the possibility of resurrection.

This laying aside has already been our experience in this last generation. The revision of the liturgy of the Church, and the changes of emphasis within our worshiping life as we have become a more openly eucharistic Church, have been welcomed by many but have brought painful losses for others. To date, those who have attempted to turn the clock back on the Prayer Book and the style of our worshiping life have found themselves swimming against an almost impossible tide.

While not denying that many signs seem to indicate that our Church is in trouble, we want to emphasize as well how some of these adversities are nudging us into new and more fruitful directions. Complaining about the Church's failures is valueless. The time has come to identify this new sense of direction, then give it a firm foundation: prayer, worship, the study of Scripture, and thoughtful theological reflection. As we undertake these things, the sort of mission and ministry to which we are being called as individuals, as spiritual communities, and as "Church" will become increasingly clear to us.

Scanning the Horizon for New Trends

Of course, serious caveats ought to be attached to each of the trends we have been tracking. The unexpected is likely to happen and we should be ready for this.

Were the Church of England to split from top to bottom over the issue of women's ordination and a schism to occur, it is possible that considerable numbers of conservative Christians would be drawn out of the Episcopal Church into a parallel North American body. If such a catastrophe were to occur, all our bets about the future of the Episcopal Church would be off!

On the other hand, the renewal movements might trigger a deeper and more penetrating revival, which in turn would resonate with the yearnings of an American people experiencing increased spiritual hunger. Such an awakening would no doubt profoundly influence other Christian traditions, and would produce not only spontaneous growth, but also a revolutionary rethinking of the relationship between the various denominations.

The scenarios are endless, and we need to be ready for surprises. Human history has taken some strange twists and turns. No one can deny that we live in extraordinary times, the unexpected having become the norm on the world scene in recent years! It is in such eras that God's hand intervenes in mysterious ways.

Once we have an idea of the trends shaping our future, it is vital that we track them to their conclusion and be on the lookout for new trends emerging. It could be that some of our trends will trickle like water into the desert sand and be lost. The important rising trends might at this moment be little more than a cloud the size of "a man's hand," but in due course they will envelop the Church with both blessing and fury.

At present, we are watching the whole issue of the family creeping up the list of American and Christian priorities. Not only are Americans attempting to define the family in light of present realities, but they are beginning to ask fundamental questions about the long-term effects on the lives of both adults and children of no-fault divorce. Rumblings in both major political parties and a growing discomfort in churches, mainline and conservative, suggest this is something that needs monitoring in the months ahead.

The rape of the environment; the impoverishment of the nations of the Two-Thirds World that live under crushing burdens of debt; the glaringly inequitable distribution of wealth; the potential for international instability as rich and poor, north and south, square off against each other—all these are bound to become a painful dimension of our global consciousness before this century ends. How we handle ourselves as a Church could quickly become a significant concern. Not only will our Christian charity be severely tested, but so will our theology. The churches could find themselves increasingly unpopular, stripped of tax privileges, and standing on their own over the issue of radical concessions being made to the world's downtrodden.

America's is an aging society, and ministry to and by the elderly could become a major point of possible growth and contention as the 1990s proceed. It is inevitable that, as the baby boomers enter the final portion of their active business lives, we will be forced to rethink many facets of our culture in light of this overload of senior citizens. Just as the baby boomers reshaped our whole approach to youth ministry, so they will affect elder ministry and elder care. This is a long-term trend about which we should already be thinking.

This last possibility raises a vital consideration: namely, that our planning can no longer be confined to a triennial basis. "Muddling through" will no longer do. As trends are identified we should be prepared to work out their implications in the life of the Episcopal Church. For example, in twenty years the first cohort of baby boomers will be retiring. Unlike today's elders, they may not receive generous checks from Social Security, and private pension plans may be facing similar difficulties. Some boomers will have saved and will be quite prosperous; others will be scraping to make ends meet. They are likely to be a fairly healthy bunch, but because of the divorce epidemic there will be a patchwork quilt of interrelationships, and huge numbers of singles will be consumed by loneliness in their "golden years."

Just as it is not too early now for boomers to be thinking about financing retirement, neither is it too early for the Episcopal Church to be giving preliminary thought to the dilemma—and opportunities for ministry—with which such a demographic avalanche is likely to present us. Maybe those of us who are clergy need to be thinking less about retirement when that time comes, and more about combining ministry to our contemporaries with a somewhat slower work-pace. There will still be social and educational needs, communities to be built, physical and social ills to which to attend in Christ's name. This might also be a time of great blessing for the Episcopal Church.

A Bright, Bright Future

Pessimists are already writing our Church's epitaph, and adding sweeping misrepresentations about our having abandoned Scripture and the Christian tradition. If you pick and choose your facts, you can paint a pretty miserable picture of any human institution, especially ours. Despite its many shortcomings, we do not share such gloom about the future of our Church. Certainly, we've got a lot of problems to solve, but there are also some exciting challenges out there waiting for us to get our teeth into them.

Change for the better does not come overnight, so we counsel patience. But when it does come, we call our fellow Christians in the Episcopal Church to gird up their loins and face the future with excitement and enthusiasm. These could be vintage years for our grand old Church!

Episcopal Trends Survey

*B*y now you will have realized *New Millennium, New Church* has not been written to entertain (although we hope you enjoyed it), but to educate, stimulate and invite your response.

Today's information technology enables us to track the developments that shape our ministry in the future, but these require constant monitoring so that forecasts can be modified in light of new data. This book could spawn a network of Episcopal Trend Trackers working together to understand the challenges thrusting us into the twenty-first century.

New Millennium, New Church was finished on October 1991, and is a snapshot of the Church that day. Trends don't stop. They're always developing, and unexpected circumstances produce all sorts of twists and turns. If this book has stimulated, intrigued or peaked your curiosity, let us know. You probably have perceptions we missed, and could help us grasp a clearer picture of the unfolding situation in the Episcopal Church.

It is important you help because these are the trends that will shape your church of the next millennium. If you would like to participate in this data-gathering and interpreting we offer you this opportunity. We hope to collect a network of observant people, lured by the promise that Episcopal trend tracking can yield priceless data to plan our future mission. Please get in touch with us at:

Episcopal Trends
c/o SPCK
P.O. Box 879
Sewanee, TN 37375-0879

We will give you the opportunity to enroll as a partner in this exciting work, keeping you regularly informed of data collected and trends discerned.

END NOTES

Notes to Chapter One

1 John M. Mulder, "The Reforming of American Presbyterianism," a paper delivered to the Executives of the Presbyterian Church (USA), Hilton Head, South Carolina, 1991.

2 Milton J. Coalter, John M. Mulder, and Louis B. Weeks, eds., *The Presbyterian Presence: The Twentieth-Century*, 7 vols. (Louisville: Westminster/John Knox Press, 1990).

3 *The Anglican Digest* (Easter 1991).

4 Tom Sine, "Shifting Christian Mission into the Future Tense," *Missiology* 11:1 (1987), p. 15.

5 George E. Barna, *The Frog in the Kettle* (Ventura: Regal Books, 1990), p. 21.

Notes to Chapter Two

1 The Gallup Organization and the Episcopal Church Center, *The Spiritual Health of the Episcopal Church* (New York, July 1989), p. 3.

2 "All state churches and national denominations, with their myriads of agencies and institutions, are now rapidly becoming permeated with charismatics." David B. Barrett, *International Bulletin of Missionary Research* 12:3 (1988), p. 119.

3 Mulder, "Reforming."

Notes to Chapter Three

1 Letter from Walter D. Dennis, August 29, 1991.

2 Ibid.

3 Terence Kelshaw, "The Bishop's Column," *The Rio Grande Episcopalian*, September 1991, p. 2.

4 The history of this period is dealt with at length in David E. Sumner's *The Episcopal Church's History: 1945-1985* (Wilton: Morehouse-Barlow, 1987), pp. 57ff.

5 Robert Wuthnow, *The Restructuring of American Religion* (Princeton: Princeton University Press, 1988), p. 156.

6 For details of the rise of Clinical Pastoral Education, see John Booty's *The Episcopal Church in Crisis* (Cambridge, MA: Cowley Publications, 1988), pp. 25-26.

7 A comparison of 1960s and 1990s issues can be found in Barna, p. 87.

8 Walter D. Dennis, "A Personal Perspective on the Episcopal Church in the 1990s," *St. Luke's Journal of Theology* (34:1):18.

Notes to Chapter Four

1 Dennis, "A Personal Perspective," p. 18.

2 George Carey, "Evangelical Fellowship in the Anglican Communion," *Bulletin* 42:1 (1991), p. 7.

3 Tex Sample, *U.S. Lifestyles and Mainline Churches* (Louisville: Westminster/John Knox, 1990), p. 69.

4 Mulder, "Reforming."

Notes to Chapter Five

1 Barna, p. 139.

2 Booty, p. 32.

3 The Community of the Holy Spirit and the Community of the Celebration.

4 "Examination of a Deacon," The Book of Common Prayer, p. 543.

5 Barna, pp. 28, 124.

6 Source: Office of Evangelism, the Episcopal Church Center.

Notes to Chapter Six

1 The Book of Common Prayer, p. 13.

2 For further reading, see William Dyrness, *Learning about Theology from the Third World* (Grand Rapids: Zondervan, 1990) and James Griffiss, *Naming the Mystery* (Cambridge, MA: Cowley Publications, 1990).

3 Booty, p. 31.

Notes to Chapter Seven

1 Gallup, p. 82.

[2] John Naisbitt and Patricia Aburdene Morrow, *Megatrends 2000* (New York: Morrow, 1990), p. 217.

[3] Barbara Brown Zikmund, "Ministry of Work and Sacrament: Women and Changing Understandings of Ordination," in *The Presbyterian Predicament: Six Perspectives*, Milton J. Coalter, John M. Mulder, and Louis B. Weeks, eds. (Louisville: Westminster/John Knox Press, 1990), pp. 98-99.

[4] Naisbitt and Morrow, p. 219.

[5] "The academic and intellectual level in seminaries would be mediocre indeed were it not for the ever-increasing number of women who, as their denominations began to allow their ordination, started coming to the seminaries in significant numbers in the 1960s." Paul Wilkes, "The Hands that Would Shape our Souls," *The Atlantic Monthly* (December 1990), p. 6.

[6] H. A. Snyder and D. V. Runyon, *Foresight* (Nashville: Thomas Nelson, 1987), pp. 108-109.

Notes to Chapter Eight

[1] Lyle E. Schaller, *It's a Different World* (Nashville: Abingdon, 1987), p. 33; Barna, p. 139.

[2] In 1950 there was one priest for every available cure; by 1990 this ratio had risen to 2:1. (source: Church Pension Fund).

[3] William S. Pregnall, *The Episcopal Seminary System During the Decline of the American Empire* (Cincinnati: Forward Movement, 1988), p. 38.

[4] Quoted in Snyder and Runyon, pp. 81-82.

[5] Barna, p. 156.

Notes to Chapter Nine

[1] Richard Walker, "The Rest Is Recent History," *The Living Church*, April 21, 1991, p. 8-9.

[2] Robert N. Bellah et al., eds., *Habits of the Heart* (New York: Harper & Row, 1986), p. 75.

[3] Sample, p. 89.

[4] Wuthnow, p. 160.

Notes to Chapter Ten

[1] David B. Barrett, *Chaos and the Gospel* (Birmingham, AL: New Hope, 1987), p. 75.

2 Resolutions of the 1988 Lambeth Conference, which is held every ten years in Canterbury.

3 Decade of Evangelism *Sharings* (1:2):1.

4 "Report of the Standing Commission on Evangelism" in *The Blue Book: Reports of the Committees, Commissions, Boards, and Agencies of the General Convention of the Episcopal Church* (New York: The Episcopal Church Center, 1991), pp. 102-103.

Notes to Chapter Eleven

1 For details of the Alabama Plan, see *Jesus, Dollars and Sense*, Oscar C. Carr, Jr., ed., (New York: Seabury Press, 1976).

2 John V. Taylor, *Enough is Enough* (London: SCM Press, 1973), p. 40.

3 Taylor, *Enough*, pp. 40ff.

4 *The Blue Book*, 1991.

5 M. Douglas Meeks, *God the Economist* (Minneapolis: Augsburg-Fortress, 1989), p. 182.

6 *Journal of Convention* (Rochester: Episcopal Diocese of Rochester, 1988), pp. 69-70.

Notes to Chapter Twelve

1 Wade Clark Roof, "The Episcopalian Goes the Way of the Dodo," *Wall Street Journal* (July 20, 1990).

2 Robert Wuthnow, *The Struggle for America's Soul* (Grand Rapids: Eerdmans, 1989), p. xii.

3 "There is reason to doubt the future effectiveness of political action and organization. Episcopalians United was created in 1987 to witness to Christian orthodoxy on morality and liturgy. Though they were both well financed and well organized and represented the opinions of most Episcopalians on sexuality, they were unable to change the outcome." Quoted from "Reflections on Phoenix," an article published by the Episcopal Synod of America, 1991, in *Foundations*.

Notes to Chapter Thirteen

1 Naisbitt and Morrow, pp. 191-192.

2 These descriptions of generational contrasts are drawn from William Straus and Neil Howe, *Generations: The History of*

America's Future 1584-2069 (New York: Morrow, 1991), pp. 261-316.

3 James L. Duncan in "Letters to the Editor," *The Living Church* (July 22, 1990).

4 What is happening in the Episcopal Church is not unlike Alvin and Heidi Toffler's description of "the decolonization of business": "Every big company today has, hidden within itself, a number of 'colonies' whose inhabitants behave like colonized populations everywhere—obedient or even servile in the presence of the ruling elite, contemptuous or resentful in its absence....The struggle to rebuild business on post bureaucratic lines is partly a struggle to decolonize the organization—to liberate these suppressed groupings. In fact, one might say that the key problem facing all big companies today is how to unleash the explosive, innovative energies of these hidden colonies." *Powershift* (New York: Bantam, 1990), p. 184.

5 Resolution B037, the General Convention of the Episcopal Church, 1991, originating with Bishop J. Winterrowd of Colorado.

6 Daniel P. Matthews, from an address to the Annual Graduate Fellowship Dinner of the Episcopal Church Foundation, January 31, 1991.

✚

Notes to Chapter Fourteen

1 Atef A. Gawad, "Moscow's Arms-for-Ore Diplomacy," *Foreign Policy* (Summer 1986), p. 147.

2 Vinay Samuel and Christopher Sugden, *Lambeth: A View from the Two-Thirds World* (London: SPCK, 1989), p. 12.

3 Gordon Aeschliman, *Global Trends* (Downers Grove: Inter-Varsity Press, 1990), p. 27.

4 Samuel and Sugden, p. 125.

5 Naisbitt and Morrow, pp. 118-119.

6 "Theology emanating from [the Third World] will in some way reflect and engage the issues of poverty, indigenous and modernizing traditions, and cultural and family pride. But the way these issues are addressed will reflect the unique history and culture of each region." Dyrness, p. 16.

*C*OWLEY PUBLICATIONS is a ministry of the Society of St. John the Evangelist, a religious community for men in the Episcopal Church. Emerging from the Society's tradition of prayer, theological reflection, and diversity of mission, the press is centered in the rich heritage of the Anglican Communion.

Cowley Publications seeks to provide books, audio cassettes, and other resources for the ongoing theological exploration and spiritual development of the Episcopal Church and others in the body of Christ. To this end, it is dedicated to developing a new generation of theological writers, encouraging them to produce timely, creative, and stimulating publications of excellence, and making these publications available widely, reaching both clergy and lay persons.